THE SAVING
POSSIBILITY

THE SAVING POSSIBILITY

a contemporary refocusing of the christian message

WILLIAM K. McELVANEY

ABINGDON PRESS
NASHVILLE and NEW YORK

THE SAVING POSSIBILITY

Copyright © 1971 by Abingdon Press

ISBN 0-687-36870-7

Library of Congress Catalog Card Number: 79-160796

Scripture quotations unless otherwise noted are
from the Revised Standard Version of the Bible,
copyrighted 1946 and 1952 by the Division of
Christian Education, National Council of Churches,
and are used by permission.

SET UP, PRINTED, AND BOUND BY THE
PARTHENON PRESS, AT NASHVILLE,
TENNESSEE, UNITED STATES OF AMERICA

To Fran

CELEBRATION IS WHEN . . .
a yellow kite soars in the
breeze

CONTENTS

CONTENTS

PREFACE

If you read this book, you will be encountering profiles and images of the gospel which refocus the
Christian message for today. Thus, this is not another critique on church renewal per se. Anyone
who has availed himself of even a glance at the
so-called religious book market is aware of the almost endless prognostications concerning the church
—its impending doom, its renewal, its last days, its
new future, its captivity, its possibility. Likewise, we
have been surfeited with writing which attempts to
formulate a contemporary case for the reality or un-
reality of God. The spectrum ranges from various
death-of-God assertions to neoclassical frameworks
vis-à-vis process philosophy, and to the assertion
that we should declare a moratorium for the foresee-
able future on the very use of the term "God."

Many, if not all, of these writings centering on
either the church or our understanding of God have
contributed to our thought in a time of theological
exploration. And these efforts, of course, have not
been unrelated to an articulation of the Christian
message itself in today's world. The essence of this
book, however, is a constructive, yet hopefully
provocative restatement of the gospel, which, if
one might put it this way, is the link between God

and the church, and for that matter, between the church and the world.

Some of my particular concerns are mirrored in questions like these: Can we claim that man's identity, meaning, and hope are truly "in God alone" without reducing the urgency of man's efforts for a more humane world? Can we be utterly motivated to work for the diminution of racism and poverty and other dehumanizing realities without attributing to the outcome of those efforts a finality and totality of meaning in and of themselves? Must the Word, which has indeed become flesh, be distorted into a fleshless Word not seriously involved in politics, economics, and the social order, or distorted into a wordless flesh which, in the name of humanitarian reform or revolution, makes a just social order a final beatitude and point of reference? Must we have a gospel of revelation without revolutionary implications? Can we settle for a gospel of revolution no longer grounded in a gospel of revelation?

I am under no illusion that I have offered herein a systematic or comprehensive answer to these questions. What I do believe I am offering is a way of looking at the gospel which can stir the imagination of you the reader to rethink the implications of the gospel for your own life and for local congregations today.

Many of us have either been preaching or listening to the gospel for most of our lives. That very fact suggests a danger to which we unconsciously become susceptible. That danger is "death" through familiarity and routine. The truth is that we tend to grow stale, one-sided, and fuzzy precisely about those matters with which we might seem to be most familiar and certain. For example, we tend to take our families for granted because we are so intertwined with each other on a daily basis. And clergymen know that the most difficult preaching texts are frequently the ones which are most familiar to our hearing, the reason being that we—supposedly—*already* know what that text has to say.

I doubt if any of us have been exempt from the disturbing experience by which we suddenly discover that our daily routine has somehow robbed us of a fresh and re-created knowledge rather than providing one. All of a sudden we realize that we have been going through the motions of whatever it is we do and that we no longer really know what's going on. I have experienced this over and over again in discussion with seminary students, through the discerning questions of the congregation I serve, or through confrontation with black churchmen. I discover that I'm not as sure as I thought I was about why I do what I do, about my rationale for making certain decisions, about my presuppositions for activities in which I have been engaged for years. Then I plunge into asking old questions anew, or asking what seems like new questions, that I should have been consciously wrestling with all along.

In some such sense we need to reexamine ourselves in our understanding and application of the Christian gospel. The purpose of this book is to be a catalyst for clergymen and laymen who want to probe anew into their perception of the gospel. While I will suggest some directions that I have found fruitful in the local parish, my basic intention

11

is to raise questions for you, the reader, so that your imagination will be set free to gain your own new perspectives on the gospel. Hopefully, you might struggle with this material together with your fellow clergymen or laymen in a way that will clarify your mutual understanding of the gospel and its meaning for your lives and for your own parish and community.

Here is an abbreviated map of our journey. Chapter 1 provides a contemporary refocusing on the gospel which I think is particularly significant in a time in which the question of man's very survival has become paramount. While not claiming to be a pooling of the diversified biblical witnesses, this material suggests an essential characteristic of the gospel which I believe is inherent in all of the New Testament writers in their witness to the gospel. This characteristic I call "The Saving Possibility."

In chapter 2 I offer sketches of a theology of celebration, affirmation, and hope. This is in no sense a systematic statement, but a battery of life-affirming images which, when pieced together, offer a somewhat composite mosaic of the gospel as I perceive it. Chapter 3 is concerned with applying the gospel in a constructive way to persons through pastoral care by laymen, a subject about which relatively little has been written. Chapter 4 reflects on the dual role of the church in today's society—the humanization of possibilities and the humanization of polarization. Finally, chapter 5 deals with a Christian affirmation of death in a way which I believe to be much more persuasive and profound than the interpretation I have usually heard in the church or, for that matter, in secular ideologies. So, we will examine the gospel through the lens of the Saving Possibility and proceed to examine the life and death implications.

On this particular occasion I'd like to thank the following persons for being who they are to me. First and most of all, my parents, Eugene and Sue Mc-Elvaney, who have given me abundant gifts to affirm; Marshall T. Steel, whose ministry and love for the church as an instrument of caring about people I have appreciated for many years; Joseph W. Mathews for his existential application of the gospel to life; Edward C. Hobbs for turning the New Testament from water into wine; to my colleagues of the ordained ranks with whom I labor, and especially Wilfred M. Bailey for his consistent integrity and openness of self; and the members of Northaven United Methodist Church, who have greatly enriched both my understanding of the gospel as well as my personal life.

I am indebted to Victor P. Furnish of the Perkins School of Theology and to Schubert M. Ogden of the University of Chicago for reading portions of the manuscript and offering suggestions for improvements which otherwise would not have been made. I also wish to express gratitude for the opportunity to deliver the 1970 Rejebian Sermons at Highland Park United Methodist Church, Dallas, during which some of the themes herein were more fully developed from outline form. A very special thanks is extended to Dotti Timmins for many hours of typing and retyping, done with both proficiency and between-the-lines care and understanding.

The Gospel Refocused: The Saving Possibility

1

Our fathers in the biblical faith were unlikely can-
didates to become our mentors of life. After all,
they were Semitic slaves in Egypt, and they did not
have much by any standard. Their qualifications for
a starring role in the self-understanding of countless
future men appeared remote indeed. They had no
great religious heritage of a conscious, continuous
nature. They had no church, no creeds, no systematic theology, no Old or New Testament. Nor
did they have Jesus. About all they had were aches
and pains from stomping straw in the sun day after
day for Pharaoh's bricks.

They became our fathers primarily *through an
event*. This event was not only a historical event
involving Semitic slaves in Egypt, but in a sense con-
stituted a revealing of life's intrinsic character in the
depths of reality. They labeled this event Exodus. It
gave birth to a community of people who began
to know themselves as a people in covenant with
God. This people faced the wilderness, the pioneer
life of the frontier, the development of a new nation, divisions, exiles, defeats, victories—all as
God's covenant people. While no one event can
embrace their total self-understanding, it was Exo-

dus which made possible the emergence of their new self-understanding as a covenant community.

Exodus: The Codeword That Every Situation Brings a Saving Possibility

Exodus, while pointing to the departure of Semitic slaves from their bondage in Egypt, also pointed beyond itself to the very metabolism of life. Exodus may be regarded as the secular, historical, and yet theological codeword, that every circumstance contains within it the door of deliverance. Somewhere in every situation there is a parting of the Red Sea, the providing of a Saving Possibility. That God is always calling men, through the events of life, out of Egypt, that is, bondage, is one way of pointing to an indispensable dimension of the good news of the Old Testament. Exodus, somewhat like creation, is not simply a past reality, but is the continual re-creation of life. Exodus is "who God is" and "what God does."

Our fathers did not arrive at their faith in God by conjuring up or inventing a deity. Life came to them, as it does to us, as event, as happening, as change. In all the vicissitudes of life, they came to realize that the gift of a Saving Possibility was always present. We should not be surprised that God was thought of as Savior or Redeemer in the biblical tradition. The mainstream of Old Testament thought represents the promise and the claim of the Saving Possibility, through which we are confronted with the source and meaning of our lives. To be sure, there is an extremely rich diversity of Old Testament witnesses who travel various routes in their spokesmanship for God. But in one way or another, they point to the promise and the claim of the Saving Possibility present in all situations.

Easter: The Re-presentation of Codeword Exodus

In the New Testament, Easter, in one sense, re-presents the reality of the codeword Exodus: the establishment of a community (the risen body of Christ) whose basic understanding of life is that, in all circumstances, a Saving Possibility is offered. While it is dangerous to indiscriminately pool the New Testament witness in the interest of a definable unity, I do believe that a common denominator among New Testament witnesses is the reality of the Saving Possibility in all the yes's and no's of life.

A central message of Jesus, particularly in Matthew and Mark, has been characterized by some New Testament scholars as the proclamation of the Reign or Rule of God.[1] If we use Romans as a characteristic statement of Paul's theology, the righteousness of God, through which men are accepted in spite of their evil, is a key theme. The cross of Jesus is a sign of God's unconditional love, which places a demand on men to let their old self-understandings die. A third major New Testament witness, the Johannine material, characteristically points to Jesus as the revealer of true life whom

[1] Rudolf Bultmann, *Theology of the New Testament* (New York: Charles Scribner's Sons, 1954), Vol. 1, chapter 1. Also, Gunther Bornkamm, *Jesus of Nazareth* (New York: Harper & Brothers, 1960), chapter 4.

God has sent and through whom men can truly have abundant life.

I cannot overemphasize that the differences in the New Testament are at least as striking as the similarities. Anyone who has compared Matthew with John, or Paul with James, does not have to be convinced of the individuality and uniqueness of each New Testament contributor. Yet are not all of these witnesses, each in his own unique style and conceptuality, pointing to the Saving Possibility present in all situations? And are not the major Christian celebrations kaleidoscopic means of pointing to the nuances of judgment-love which constitute the Saving Possibility in all events? This theme of the Saving Possibility neither embraces nor exhausts the important differences within the New Testament. It is, however, a thread that runs through them all.

Whether Orthodox, Roman Catholic, or Protestant, the historical witness of the Christian community has revolved around various interpretations of the Exodus-Easter theme of the Saving Possibility. Easter is the New Testament confirmation that even the most impossible situation contains the seeds of a Saving Possibility. For after all, as Paul Tillich once put it, Christian faith was born in the grave. Out of death came life, out of darkness came light, out of hopelessness came hope, out of rejection came resurrection. It is no wonder that Easter is the ultimate Christian celebration, for it is the final affirmation and confirmation that the intrinsic nature of life is a Saving Possibility.

In order to appreciate Easter as the ultimate re-presentation of the Saving Possibility of God in all situations, we need greater clarity than the church has usually provided. Specifically, the *meaning* of the empty tomb stories in the Gospels and the *message* of the risen Christ within that overall meaning need to be refocused in order to do justice to the stories themselves and to the universal experience of mankind.

The usual literal interpretation of the empty tomb stories in the four Gospels as the resuscitation of Jesus' body obscures the true significance of Easter by removing the reality of the cross. The crucifixion of Jesus, who for the disciples was the essence and epitome of their hopes and expectations, necessitated the disciples' most radical decision. One alternative was to crumble as victims of life, to conclude that life was no longer a possibility. One expects that for a while after the crucifixion they despaired of life itself, feeling that they had received the sentence of death.

In fact, it is surprising how seldom the church has looked at the disciples after the crucifixion through the microscope of an actual, real-life understanding of grief. All too often we have obscured the disciples' real choice at this point with an aura of miracle, mystery, and magic. In their grief over the loss of Jesus and of their various expectations related to him, they would have experienced shock and disbelief; anger with life, themselves, and those who were most directly involved with the crucifixion; disorganization and uncertainty; and personal guilt. The church's tradition of the three days following his crucifixion and prior to the resurrection should be seen as poetry, as symbolic of the grief process working itself through.

As time elapsed, and as they examined their grief, another alternative became clearer. It was the dawning conviction that the meaning of Jesus in his teachings and in his life-style was either eternally true or else false, and that his death placed a claim upon them to decide which was the case. Somewhat like the assassination of Martin Luther King, Jr., some of us were forced to make a decision. Either life was no longer vital or worth living, or else the death commanded us to pick up our lives and redouble the deceased's efforts as our own with the confidence that the truth is its own victory and own reward. Christianity was conceived in an ignoble birth and born in an ignominious death which confronted men with a stark decision: resignation and despair due to man's evil or joyous discovery of God's Saving Possibility, even in the death of our dearest hopes and expectations. The disciples chose the latter, and in that choice was the genesis of the Christian community and its gospel for mankind.

Following the crucifixion, we might say that the disciples saw Jesus in a new way. Instead of not seeing him anywhere, they began to see him everywhere. Instead of his absolute absence, they began to perceive his total presence . . . in the breaking of bread, on the road, at their work. Jesus became the universal Christ whose indelible imprint was placed on all of creation, in all things, places, and faces. As Karl Barth once put it, "What is known and found in Jesus is that God is found everywhere." [2]

[2] Karl Barth, *Der Römerbrief,* pp. 72-73. Quoted by Schubert

As an early Christian confession puts it (used in Acts 2), "God raised him up, having loosed the pangs of death, because it was not possible for him to be held by it . . . God has made him both Lord and Christ, this Jesus whom you crucified."

Jesus, then, was set free to be the authentic, universal, eternal Christ, the event of God's graciousness toward men. His truth was irrepressible. It could not be buried. He told us that our past failures need not be the final story of our lives and that the future offered a new choice. Can that be buried? Can any grave contain the truth that all men are of equal worth in the eyes of God and thus deserve to be treated as human beings? Can assassination or crucifixion, call it what you will, destroy the reality that whatever a person sows that shall he reap, in terms of life's meaning and quality? Truth cannot be locked in a tomb.

Is it any wonder that Christian symbols of the resurrection include the imagery of being set free? Consider the eagle, the dolphin, and the butterfly. In short, what was revealed to the disciples was that what Jesus was, what he taught, the way he lived, were the very truths of creation re-presented for all men. It was true in the beginning, is now, and ever shall be. This is the *real* meaning of the empty tomb stories, of the risen Jesus, of his various appearances to the disciples, of the ascension, elevation, or exaltation of Jesus to the "right hand of God."

Easter not only meant that the disciples saw Jesus

M. Ogden, *Christ Without Myth* (New York: Harper & Brothers, 1961), p. 10.

in a new way. They also saw themselves in a new way. They saw that they could live their lives come what may, because in spite of their own failures as well as the evil of others, God was faithful, always coming to give back the life they thought they had lost. Through the crucifixion the disciples learned that God is always giving back the life we have distorted, fouled up, or let slip away from us. They saw themselves as recipients of the Saving Possibility of a new future, and realized that all experience has this transcendent yet personal gift within it.

Easter became the codeword that God is always faithful in providing a Saving Possibility. As Barth put it, "We see the faithfulness of God remaining firm even though the noblest human hopes and expectations are dashed to the ground . . . The faithfulness of God is the answer to all human hope and desire and striving and waiting . . ." [3] Easter is the Good News that a Saving Possibility is given, even amidst the crucifixion of our fondest hopes and our deepest expectations. In other words, the truth of God's gift of a Saving Possibility cannot be overcome, and this truth can become the strength and motivation of our lives.

I have suggested that the deepest *meaning* of the empty tomb narratives in the four Gospels is the gift in all circumstances of the Saving Possibility. We now turn our attention to the *message* or the claim within that meaning. Why the church has so frequently interpreted Easter as having to do primarily with our continued subjective existence beyond life

[3] Karl Barth, *The Epistle to the Romans* (New York: Oxford University Press, 1953), trans. from sixth ed., p. 95.

as we know it here and now is indeed a mystery insofar as we look to the Gospel narratives. Not once —I repeat—not even on one occasion in any of the four Gospels does the risen Jesus so much as mention some future existence. He speaks of only one concern: *mission.*

In Matthew 28, Jesus speaks of the work of the disciples or faith community in continuing his work. "Go therefore and make disciples of all nations, baptizing them in the name of the Father and of the Son and of the Holy Spirit. . . ." The fact that this passage may be a later addition by the church simply fortifies the point that the resurrection was seen, not as an assurance of heavenly treasure in the sense of future privileges, but as a call to be the ongoing body of Christ in the world. The essentials are the same in Mark's account of the risen Lord, where in certain texts and versions Jesus commands the disciples to preach the gospel to the whole creation. Jesus speaks to the faith community about being faithful in its task, not to individuals about their subjective continued existence.

In Luke's Gospel, the risen Lord appears on the road to Emmaus, breaks bread and eats fish with the company of his friends, and calls them to be witnesses to the truth of the gospel. Even though Luke is more "physiological" than either Matthew or Mark, the missional emphasis is very much present (. . . that repentance and forgiveness should be preached in his name to all nations . . . 24:47). The fourth evangelist presents the risen Lord as one who sends the disciples on his mission (20:21-22). Also, in Chapter 21, which some scholars believe to be an addition to the original text, the fourth Gospel high-lights a missional thrust. Three times Peter is asked by Jesus whether or not Peter loves him. Peter's consistent yes is met by Jesus' insistence: Feed my lambs. Tend my sheep. Feed my sheep. There is no mention of some other world, no inference by Jesus that the meaning of his risen appearance has to do with our own personal "future life" in some other time, space, or place.

The recurring meaning of the resurrection narratives is clear: our life is in and through God who offers us himself as the Saving Possibility in all situations, and who calls us to love and be concerned with our fellowmen as God himself is. Likewise clear is the meaning of resurrection passages in Luke 24 and in John 20 and 21 where Jesus appears and disappears, encounters and then vanishes from sight. These are not hocus-pocus "now-you-see-me-now-you-don't" stories. They are, as a matter of fact, very descriptive of the precise way we find life. We are forever skeptical about the sustaining nature of life, about whether or not a Saving Possibility will be offered. In short, we are all doubting Thomases. We live by faith, and then we are faithless. We accept God's all-encompassing grace, and then we reject it. We see, and then we are blind again. We are open to others, and then we are closed. We live, and then life eludes us.

In other words, the appearances of Jesus are occasions of faith by which we truly know our identity and our destiny as those who live and move and have our being in God. We again and again think that the end of our world, so to speak, is upon us.

Easter means that God is embracing you in all ups and downs, all yes's and no's, that in the deepest and most ultimate sense you are taken care of! Easter, then, is a gospel of revelation (a Saving Possibility is given) and a call to mission, a gospel with revolutionary implications.

Now we must examine the purpose of the Saving Possibility, and follow that with the shape of the Saving Possibility.

The Saving Possibility: Saved for What?

In all situations a Saving Possibility is provided. Life always comes as a Saving Possibility. Of course, I have, more often than not, failed to see or to grasp the Saving Possibility given in my situation. But life always bears this gift, whether I see it or not. As I have attempted to point out, the Exodus-Easter theme communicates this basic, everlasting Good News. The problem, of course, is that the Saving Possibility I want or would have chosen is often not the one which is offered. In that case we are likely to conclude that no possibility is even present. This condition may be called sin, bondage, or even death. But fortunately for us God does not necessarily save us for our personal preferences most of the time. Our "druthers" are not the final criteria of what is truly saving, and for that we should thank God.

God saves us not for our own inclinations and self-styled blueprints for life, but *for himself, for our own deepest or true selves, and for our neighbor.* In our day of incredible and accelerated change, the one constant amidst it all is the certainty of God's Saving Possibility, understood in the above three-fold formula. No matter what man does in the future—even nuclear war, control of the life process through biochemistry, the overpollution and over-population of the biosphere—the reality of the Saving Possibility remains secure. Man may become involved in still more massive and terrible sufferings and terrors than we have so far known, but even this will not overcome the Saving Possibility that is God's all-embracing love for the world. Man's inhumanity to man may render our awareness and appropriation of God's Saving Possibility more and more difficult. Man's greed and indifference may inflict unimaginable suffering and hardship, but the powers and principalities of men cannot eliminate the Saving Possibility itself.

God saves us *for himself* in the sense that our own lives cannot finally be understood apart from our relationship to the Whole of life in which we live and move and have our being. When Christian faith has spoken of man living "for the glory of God," what else could be meant than the fact that man's life is related to the all-embracing Whole of reality and that each life makes an unending difference to that Whole (God). Thus, while each human being is unique or unrepeatable and of infinite worth, he is so only in relationship to the all-embracing Whole in which each person can become who he is in the first place.

While I will not try to articulate in detail man's relationship to the Whole of reality, it is clear that this relationship is one way of getting at a key

25

difference between humanism and Christian faith. In the many forms of humanism, man is, in one way or another, the final value, the ultimate point of reference, the center of all that is. For Christian faith, that all-in-all, that center, that final point of reference which constitutes the source, matrix, and meaning of man's life is the all-encompassing Whole, the inclusive Life, or God. Every man's life is understood in Christian faith as a unique part of this Whole, and his meaning is finally grounded in this Whole and becomes forever a part of it.

When we claim, then, that God saves us for himself instead of our own preferences, we are saying that our lives, whatever they are qualitatively and quantitatively, must always be seen in their wider relationships to the Whole. We are inferring that the true glory of every life is in its affirmation and resulting relationship to other human beings and to the all-encompassing Whole in which all human beings are sustained and have their final everlasting meaning. For a much more extensive treatment of the relationship of the individual to the Whole, I refer the reader to the works of Charles Hartshorne, such as *Man's Vision of God,* and to the writings of Schubert M. Ogden, specifically *The Reality of God.*[4]

Through the Saving Possibility offered in all situations, God saves us not only for himself, but also

---

[4] Charles Hartshorne, *Man's Vision of God* (Hamden, Conn.: Archon Books, 1964). Also, Schubert M. Ogden, *The Reality of God* (New York: Harper & Row, 1964). Other pertinent works of Hartshorne are *Reality as Social Process* (New York: The Free Press, 1953), and *The Divine Relativity* (New Haven: Yale University Press, 1964).

for our deepest and truest selves. The truth of this assertion becomes more evident by analyzing the vicissitudes of life. As we look at life on the surface, there seems to be conflicting evidence as we ask the question, "Is life good?" or "What makes life good?" No one has to be convinced of the abundance of the "life is no good" evidence. We are all but inundated with the "bad" news of life . . . war, physical and psychological violence, poverty, pollution, racial and class hatreds, injustices and exploitation, concentration camps, loneliness and suffering, mass starvation, national catastrophes and all the rest.

On the other hand is the apparent "life is good" evidence. It too is lengthy and astonishing. The sheer wonder of being and the mystery of the universe. The growing discovery of self. The beauty of relationships, the grace of the I-Thou. The miracle of the seasons, the loveliness of a mountain harebell, the rushing noise of a mountain stream in the wilderness. The joy of achievement, the freshness of experience. The timelessness of great music, the freedom of the dance, the creativity of the arts. Love. A cold glass of water on a hot day. The gift of a new beginning. Great causes. The miracle and marvel of children.

It seems that we have two sets of evidence. Shall we conclude that life is good for some people and not for others? Or, as far as we ourselves are concerned, that life is good part of the time and not good at other times? Certainly, on the emotional level we feel this way again and again. The heart of the matter resides in the criterion to be used in determining whether life is good or not. Is our criterion whether or not we, so to speak, get what we want? The trouble with that is that we often do not know what is good for us, and this is proven again and again in retrospect.

If our ultimate criterion is ease, comfort, or absence of suffering, this too exposes our limited wisdom. For universal experience has proven that some who have dealt with great hardships and disappointments have more internal peace, greater self-understanding, and more concern for others than those who have had a comparatively easy and comfortable life. There are no automatic limits to the capacity of human beings in becoming their deepest and truest selves, even in the most trying circumstances. Viktor Frankl made just this point in *Man's Search for Meaning* when he claimed that the last privilege of the prisoner was his self-determination, whether he would suffer with as much dignity and as little hatred as possible, or else surrender all vestiges of being a human being.[5] We cannot say what we would do under such circumstances. We can only point to the certainty that, even in the worst situations, a Saving Possibility is offered by which we can lay hold of our most real and human selves.

As we look at the sufferings of so many people— disease, hunger, humiliation, injustices—it is very difficult to avoid the conclusion that some people do seem to get dealt a better hand than others in the finitude and freedom of the life process. Yet, at the same time, we see the marks of death on

[5] (New York: Washington Square Press, 1963).

those who live in ease and comfort: an affluent society increasingly accustomed to illusion through drugs, a people increasingly dependent on military "solutions," repression of minority groups, widespread family and personal instability, a society driven by an earth-destroying consumer technology, and a malaise of meaning about life itself. These facts preclude us from concluding that only in affluent situations is there a Saving Possibility at hand. No, whether in suffering or out, the Saving Possibility graces our lives with the invitation to become our deepest and truest selves, selves who refuse to surrender the affirmation of life, who are as concerned for the life of others as circumstances allow, and who believe in the significance of their own lives in relationship to the Whole.

God saves us not only for himself and for our real selfhood, but also *for our neighbor*. For we cannot even become our deepest and most profound selves apart from concern for others. Our concern for the needs of others in terms of food, housing, education, and employment is our participation in God's creation so as to point to that ultimate ground of grace in which our total lives have their ultimate meaning. So when we, by whatever means, make it possible for the hungry to obtain food, for the homeless to be cared for, for the powerless to help themselves, we are partners with God in the ongoingness of his creation. At the same time, we are witnessing to the reality of re-creation or redemption, which constitutes God's gift of himself to all men, by which we discover our true identity, purpose, and destiny.

It was Alexander Miller who wrote that "to give

men bread is not to affirm that they live by bread alone, but to witness that we do not." Thus, in meeting another's needs for the essentials of food and clothing, we do more than meet these needs. We are in fact responding to the most profound need of all men, namely, for an understanding of how to be and to act as a human being. Affluent America would be a paradise of humanity instead of a confused, defensive, and frightened conglomerate of society if bread alone could suffice for man.

Thus, God saves us for our neighbor in two ways. One is by freeing us to meet the physical and immediate hunger of our neighbor. The other is by pointing, in the very act of meeting his immediate need, to the Bread of life by which we are sustained in all circumstances. To fail to do either of these is to fail both ourselves and our neighbors. For in ministering to our neighbor, we further open the door of his possibility in likewise ministering to his neighbor.

Before proceeding, I must say that I have great respect for the claim made, for example, in Colin Morris' *Unyoung-Uncolored-Unpoor* that love is largely the prerogative of those who have enough to eat. "The present system makes it impossible for millions to love their neighbor. . . . Love, compassion, and forgiveness have no place in the animal world, and that is where the majority of mankind lives." [6] Human beings who are forced to constantly grub for food have little opportunity for concern about others, and, as Morris asserts, the majority of the

[6] (Nashville: Abingdon Press, 1969), pp. 146-47.

world is now in this condition, with the prospects for the future yet more grim.

The point I must make absolutely clear here is that our first responsibility to persons who are hungry is to put bread into their stomachs, and I don't mean some kind of spiritual bread. We must be equally clear, however, that when ample food, clothing, housing, and even opportunity are unquestionably available, none of these ensures in and of itself an abundant life in the biblical sense of that term.

I cannot agree with Morris when he asserts that "*only* [italics mine] free men can enter the Kingdom of God." [7] Without depreciating one iota the significance of political freedom, such freedom cannot be equated with the Kingdom of God. To suppose otherwise is to say that freedom is God. Furthermore, who is really willing to claim that there were no men of faith in Hitler's Germany, or in South Africa today? The sufficient presence of the material necessities of creation is a sacramental reminder that we do not live by bread alone, but by the re-creation of human life grounded in the all-embracing love of God. That is why I sometimes offer as a Eucharistic call to worship this phrase: "Today we use bread to be reminded that we do not live by bread alone, but by every gift that comes from God."

By now it should be clear that the Saving Possibility is not some placebo or palliative from the realm of positive thinking, nor a man-made possi-

[7] *Ibid.*, p. 147.

bility on his own terms. Instead, the Saving Possibility is based on the reality that man's source and meaning are in his relationship to God, that what we want or prefer is not necessarily what comes to us, and that there is not a fully realized appropriation of God's Saving Possibility for our lives apart from our concern for our neighbor. The Saving Possibility carries a demand or claim which is firmly implanted in the gift or promise.

Shapes of Saving Possibilities

How does Exodus come to us? What does Easter look like in our lives? I will not attempt a systematic answer, but rather some thought-provoking directions. I'll suggest that there are two shapes of the Saving Possibility which are signs and seals of God's unconditional love, but which point beyond themselves to God's love itself as the final source of all Saving Possibility.

circumstantial change

Some Saving Possibilities occur in the shape of what I call *circumstantial change*. Our external circumstances change in a way that offers new hope, new responses, new potential, a new future. The primary biblical understanding of Exodus was the involvement of God in a historical event which brought about a radical change of circumstances in the lives of a people who were slaves under Pharaoh. One can interpret Exodus in many ways, but it represented a liberation of a group of Semitic slaves from their dehumanizing situation under Pharaoh.

External changes in circumstances may include individuals or groups of persons and will almost surely involve decisions, participation, and risk. Circumstantial change as a life-giving Exodus may come about in many ways. We have seen some advances, for example, in the 1960's in civil rights, which offered possibilities previously denied. On the individual level we sometimes have seen a change in work or in family environment literally transform a person's self-understanding and sense of well-being.

As I see the church, it is called to be a Word-bearing change agent which exists both to bear a Word about the source, meaning, and destiny of all life, as well as to serve as an agent of individual and social change. The church is more than a vision keeper and proclaimer, and more than a social action organization. It is a community of both Word and Deed, the two being so inseparable that we might spell it out as the community of the _wordeed_.

The _wordeed_ of the community of Christ is the grace-prompted task of discerning the openings in history which are given, and to move into those openings as God's ally for the freeing of those who are bound. This task is one of bringing about changes in external circumstances, of being co-operating agents in a contemporary Exodus from bondage to new possibilities. These changes may include low-cost housing, fair housing, day-care centers, job opportunities, individual rights, educational opportunities, emergency loan funds, and an almost endless list of other involvements which change the circumstances of people's lives.

Chapter 4 will devote additional space and effort to these possibilities. At this point I simply want to make it clear that the Christian community not involved to the hilt in these Exodus events is, at best, peripheral to the deepest needs of our time, and at worst, an escape from the world. As one statement of theological training expressed it, the church "must quiet her answers to questions no one is asking, until, in taking the agony of the world on herself, she becomes the cruciformed answer to questions that must be asked."

As I consider the church as an agent of Exodus, of circumstantial change, I must say that there is much in James Cone's *Black Theology and Black Power* which is a hammer of truth for the white community and the white church. Systemic white violence, both overt and covert, has determined the shape of American life and history and continues to do so. The white church has been and is tragically involved in racist structures and practices. The liberal white community does expect integration and reconciliation to be on white terms, namely, a relationship of white Thous to black Its. We expect black people to love us by being what we want them to be instead of who they choose to be and confronting us with that choice. We tolerate existing violence of many kinds against blacks, yet deplore violence on their part. We define love apart from justice and power for black people and expect blacks to accept our definition.

Can there be any doubt——whether we like it or

not—that Cone is correct when he identifies the gospel with being black in the sense of being on the side of the oppressed? His words are:

To be black means that your heart, your soul, your mind, and your body are where the dispossessed are. We all know that a racist structure will reject and threaten a black man in white skin as quickly as a black man in black skin. . . . Therefore, being reconciled to God does not mean that one's skin is physically black. It essentially depends on the color of your heart, soul, and mind. . . . The real questions are: Where is your identity? Where is your being? Does it lie with the oppressed blacks or with the white oppressors? [8]

The church, white or black, which does not hear and abide by these tenets of black theology is a dispenser of a fleshless word that is an offense to God-in-Christ. If the church is to take love seriously, it must be more concerned with encouraging a shared power for the enablement of human beings in today's society and less involved with endorsing unilateral forms of power which exist primarily for enforcement. Love divorced from a concept of self-determining power is mere paternalism. As a response to paternalism, we should note carefully that the cry today is not "Black Love," "Brown Love," or "Student Love," but "Black Power," "Brown Power," and "Student Power." The disadvantaged and downtrodden have had enough so-called Christian love directed at them which does not bring

[8] James H. Cone, *Black Theology and Black Power* (New York: The Seabury Press, 1969), pp. 151-52.

with it a new share of power, dignity, and enablement. Genuine Christian love insists on a distribution of power insofar as possible.

attitudinal change

A second shape of the Saving Possibility might be called *attitudinal change*. Here we are speaking of an internal "Exodus" which frees us within a certain set of circumstances which are not changeable. These are often among the greatest triumphs in life, and they occur on many levels as a witness to the truth of the always-present Saving Possibility. What I am calling attitudinal change may also be called faith, a posture by which we decide that we can live our lives in any and all circumstances, including those which we are powerless to change.

I recall a not untypical counseling session with a young man whose wife had deserted him. They had met in Germany several years ago where he was stationed in the Armed Forces. Returning to this country three years ago, they became parents of a son. It seems that she had expressed a desire to return to Germany for a visit with her family. To make this possible, the husband saved enough money for his wife and their two-year-old son to make the trip to Germany. After several weeks had elapsed, he received a note from her stating that she was not coming back, but was remaining in her native land with the baby.

In hearing his story, I concluded that it was futile to even try to alter the circumstances of the situation. His only constructive alternative was to accept the situation and pick up his life again. Of course, this was easier to say than to do, but it is not unlike many choices that we have to face at one time or another——an unfortunate situation that cannot be changed, past failures which cannot be erased but which can be accepted, a loss of a loved one or perhaps the prospect of our own prolonged illness, including the likelihood of a terminal sickness.

In unchangeable circumstances, our attitudinal change or our acceptance of the situation becomes the shape of God's Saving Possibility. And sometimes we come to realize that our greatest problem all along has not been the circumstances in which we have been living, but our attitude about those circumstances. A colleague in the ordained ministry recently shared with a group the way he had functioned under a victim image during the first ten years of his pastorates. He had blamed the congregation, blamed his wife, found endless fault with the hierarchy, and generally made himself and others miserable. Finally, he said he became aware that some of the problem was in himself, in his own attitudes about others. During those ten years, that Saving Possibility was always there, even though he was blind to its presence. His Saving Possibility was not so much in a different congregation, a changed wife, and more progressive church leadership as in a new understanding of himself.

Sometimes we recognize the Saving Possibility when we are willing to receive the future as a new gift, regardless of our past failures and errors. As a pastor, and as a human being, I have become convinced that there is no greater handicap for

37

people than a recurring sense of failure about their lives. Like a ubiquitous smog, this sense of failure seems to envelop the lives of people and obscure their God-given possibilities. Some are convinced that they are failures as parents. "We failed to equip our children the way we had hoped to do," some say. Others are convinced that they are failures in their vocations, or in their marriages, or in other personal relationships. The result of this abiding sense of failure is either the intimidation and paralysis of people, or else we see the emergence of a dogmatic, absolutist personality, born of a sense of failure and the resulting erosion of a sense of self-worth.

There are real failures in the lives of all of us about which we can do nothing as far as correcting them or changing the consequences. For example, it takes some of us a long time to "grow up," and by the time we even begin to arrive with some maturity of our own, our children are already raised and out on their own. We wish we could start our parental responsibilities anew with the insights and intentions we now have. We wish we could start all over again. But we can't. We could say the same things about our marriages, our vocations, and various personal relationships. We cannot live it all over again, because life does not give us that choice.

There is only one redemptive thing that we can do as we consider our failures of the past. And that is to hear the gospel. The gospel comes to us as the Word that the past is received, whatever it has been, and the future comes as God's new gift for our rebirth and fulfillment. The gospel comes to us as the Word that we are free to fail—free to receive the future as a new possibility, as a sign of God's forgiveness in relation to our past. The gospel says to us in effect, "Whatever your past has been, it's all right. So you failed. All is embraced, all is forgiven, and all is received. Now live your life for the future." We all have our personal failure list, and I'm sure that mine alone could fill the rest of this book.

The gospel attacks our paralysis, our self-pity, our self-indulging, by confronting us with a question. The question is, "In what do you finally trust?" If our final trust is in the gospel of God's all-encompassing love, then our past failures cannot bury us, no matter how big and how bad our failures have been. We are free to pick up our pallet and walk and live our lives, as the Scripture puts it. Let the past be received. Accept what it was and is, and move into the new future which God is now giving you. For when we truly receive the Word that the past is received, and that we are free to fail, we are becoming, so to speak, successes in our failures. If our final trust is in the gospel rather than in images of us held by others, if we trust in the gospel instead of some idealized life plan which we refuse to give up, then we can live our lives in any and all circumstances.

There is no past which can hold us in bondage as long as our number-one trust is in the gospel. The gospel assures us that we are in fact always free to fail and free to live in a new future. To receive this Word is never easy, but no matter how difficult it may be, the gospel is calling you to become a success in your failures by receiving the future as a brand new gift.

I'm convinced that bondage to our past expresses itself in essentially two disguises. I call one of these *The Charlie Brown Disguise or Self-Image.* We all probably have some affinity for good 'ole Charlie Brown, because something of him is in so many of us. The Charlie Brown Image is fundamentally a Victim Image. Do you ever play a game known as "Ifitis"? If only I had come from different parents! If only I had a different spouse, or didn't have one at all, or did have one! If only my boss weren't such a jerk! If only our bishops had my vision of the church! If only I were more attractive—or had more money—or a different position—or some other circumstances than the ones I have! The givenness of my life is just too much!

The Charlie Brown Self-Image makes us a *prisoner* of the way things are. It is a kind of paralysis which convinces us we are helpless victims of life's circumstances. When reality is really confronted, it is more than the Charlie Brown in us can cope with most of the time.

The second disguise of bondage to our past is— and wouldn't you know it—*The Lucy Disguise or Self-Image.* Lucy is not so much a prisoner as she is a *pretender.* She is a pretender of incredible glory and power. Instead of reality making us fold up as a helpless victim, the Lucy in us pretends that the way things are is not really the way things are, that what is given is something other than what is really given. So Lucy—whether the one in Schulz's cartoon or the one in us—opts for a make-believe world. The correct name for this life of pretending is *illusion*. "I can do anything better than you," asserts Lucy, shaking her fists. Why, Lucy can put everyone down and manage to call attention to her prowess and power! She is the worldly wise fussbudget who is going to get her way. Actually, she has decided that reality is too limiting, so she makes up her own expansive universe in which to live.

As in the case of most seeming opposites, the Charlie Brown Image and the Lucy Image are strikingly similar. In terms of classical Christian theology, the Charlie Brown disguise settles for less than we could become, for less than we were made to be. This is sloth, as we have been reminded so well recently by churchmen like Harvey Cox. On the other hand, the Lucy disguise tries to be more than we can be, more than we were created to be. This is false pride, as we have been so well reminded by churchmen like Reinhold Niebuhr. Most of what the church has had to say through the years about inauthentic existence, or sin, fits into one of these two self-images.

Do you see yourself in these images which I'm holding before you? And what do you see? Perhaps some of us see a Charlie Brown on the inside and a Lucy on the outside. I suspect that if each one of us looks honestly into this mirror, we will see glimpses of one or the other, and maybe—just maybe—a silhouette of both. For after all, there really isn't much difference between a prisoner and a pretender.

When we size ourselves up, this is where we are

41

likely to be—either the self-image of Prisoner Charlie or else of Pretender Lucy. The gospel as Saving Possibility comes as a Counter-Image, saying to us, "Charlie. Lucy. Charlie-Lucy. Are you listening? Your past is O.K., with all your failures and hang-ups. Not because you can make it O.K. or because it was right or righteous. No. That is precisely what you cannot do. God gives you a Saving Possibility in the shape of a free rebirth for a new beginning. Your past no longer holds your life in its prisoner and pretender images. So live."

Sometimes the gospel enables us not only to be free *from* the past but, in a very real sense, to be free *for* the past as well. The past cannot just be erased as though it never existed. Either it controls us in a demonic way, or we learn and grow from it, thus using it as an enabler for the future. The gospel can enable us to use our past failures, so that the past no longer becomes our stumbling block to the future, but instead becomes our building block for the future, providing the raw material for our profoundest insights into our own lives and into human nature in general. When this happens, we are truly taking hold of life, and are becoming successes in our failures. Some of the greatest blindnesses, failures, and weaknesses of our past can become avenues through which we develop our most significant forms of service to others. The constructive and humane use of our past failures requires courage and continual effort, but it can result in the most gratifying experiences we know in life.

I'm thinking, for example, of a man who at one

time was an alcoholic. Over a period of time in his work with Alcoholics Anonymous he became one of the greatest assets to other alcoholics in his community. He began to use his past as an instrument of service for his fellowmen. This is what I mean by becoming free for your past, and discovering the always-present Saving Possibility. Or, I think of Anton Boisen, who wrote the book *Out of the Depths.* It was a pioneer study on the frontier of religion and psychology, and helped pave the way for clinical pastoral training in seminaries. He wrote this book after experiencing the depths of severe psychosis and a long struggle back to health. He began to use the trauma and sorrow and tragedy of his past as a building block to the future. His worst experience became his instructor rather than his incapacitator. When we do that, we are becoming successes in our failures, and we are appropriating the Saving Possibility offered to us.

The fact that God saves us for himself, for our real selves, and for our neighbors through circumstantial and attitudinal change means that no life is really defeated, no situation is hopeless, because in every situation a Saving Possibility is given. I would not, of course, suggest that we can reduce the New Testament witness to this one assumption. The New Testament witness is much too rich and varied to allow for the creation of a simplistic, synthetic unity. But I do suggest that the reality of a Saving Possibility in all situations is inherent in the various facets of the New Testament word about life. The Saving Possibility is, in one sense, what the Old Testament and New Testament witnesses are "getting at" in their many individual styles and directions.

It is apparent that if we are to receive God's Saving Possibility in some situations, there will have to be what amounts to a death of our former blueprints and wishes related to our lives. This willingness to receive the Saving Possibility which is given presupposes a trust in God's love and a giving-up of many dreams, plans, and expectations. In other circumstances, our confidence in God's Saving Possibility may mean that we refuse to accept unjust and inhumane conditions as the way it must be, so that we commit ourselves anew to being agents of Exodus in behalf of mankind. Paul might have called either of these responses a form of obedience. Jesus might have used the word repentance. Luther might have seen these responses as signs of trust. Whatever label we use, these responses are the life-style of faith in God's Saving Possibility.

The Source of All Saving Possibilities: The Love of God

So far I have sketched out two shapes of the Saving Possibility, circumstantial and attitudinal. But we must go deeper into the ultimate shape of the Saving Possibility. This reflection was drawn out in sharp relief by a Methodist layman who in a discussion group posed the question, "What is the Saving Possibility for the thousands of Biafran children who starved to death?" Related questions followed, but this particular inquiry reaches the heart of the matter. We could certainly multiply this question with many others like it.

The suffering of the innocent, particularly children, causes us to proceed to the first and last reality in which both circumstantial and attitudinal change are rooted. In the case of the Biafran children, to use that example, there was no circumstantial change as Saving Possibility. They literally starved to death by the thousands. Nor in the case of small children can we speak of a conscious and self-aware attitudinal change in the sense of a faith posture possible for adults. Where, then, is the so-called Saving Possibility?

We could assert that tragedies of this nature place a claim on us for a more responsible relationship to our fellowman, somewhat like the claim of the cross or of an assassinated leader. If so, this might come to us as a Saving Possibility, but it still doesn't help those who have already starved to death. We might also philosophize that in a finite world where men are given freedom of choice and action, the price of freedom is the possible misuse of that freedom to the detriment, or even destruction, of others. We could surmise that without that freedom there could be no meaning of any kind for mankind. After all, robots do not have personal meaning. All of this makes sense on one scale of thinking, but the question remains: What about the children who starved? Where is *their* Saving Possibility?

I do not believe we can answer this question without returning to the earlier assertion that God saves us finally for himself. When Paul tells us that neither death nor life, nor powers nor principalities can separate us from the love of God in Christ

(Romans 8), or when the author of Acts remarks that in God we live and move and have our being (Acts 17:28), they are pointing to the ultimate Saving Possibility, namely, the unconditional, everlasting love of God for all of his creation and creatures.

If, in fact, man is his own final center of value, then we must say forthrightly that the death of innocent children is a complete and final tragedy in which there is absolutely no saving quality so far as the children themselves are concerned. If so, we must be prepared to say something similar about man's life as a whole, since the illustration of children's deaths underscores the kind of apparent injustices and unfairness of life which abounds all around us. Keep in mind, however, that premature death, or seemingly unfulfilled life, for whatever reason, is finally and absolutely tragic only if man himself is the ultimate and complete point of reference for the meaning of reality.

If, however, our meaning is in God, that is, if God himself is the all-inclusive Life of Being and Becoming, the all-embracing Whole, then our lives are seen to be parts of the Whole. No part of the Whole is lost or destroyed, because it is received into the eternal life of God himself where each life makes its own unending difference in the life of God. Everything in the creation, in spite of its own finitude, is sustained in the life of God.

This realization cannot, of course, be a substitute for human sorrow or even feelings of rage and frustration—as in the case of starving children, for example. And certainly it cannot be a substitute for responsible care and action. However, the recognition that God's love is both the object and the ground of Christian hope can prevent the repeat of earlier mistaken assumptions—namely, that man can somehow get better and better and in the process build the perfect city of man. No matter how well intentioned such assumptions may be, they will lead to disillusionment if man's past experience has anything to teach us.

Theology seems apt to forget . . . that although Christian hope does indeed have to do with this world, and thus is open to all that secularity itself can hope for, it nevertheless is not in this world, but in the boundless love embracing it that such hope has its sole ground and object. For while fully affirming man's secular hope, it does not make this its only or even its primary affirmation. Its first witness, rather, is to the ultimate reality of God's love, which alone embraces not only our future in this world but also our transience, our death, and our sin, and thus creates that "hope against hope" by which, as we may believe, all men . . . are finally sustained.[9]

The ultimate Saving Possibility, then, is God's boundless and all-embracing love for his world and all his creatures. This love is the source of man's love for life and for his neighbors, as well as man's sense of hope about his own meaning and destiny. Even where there is no possibility for either circum-

[9] "Faith, Hope, and Love: Reflections on the Essence of Christianity," The Northaven Lectures in Contemporary Theology and Culture, given by Schubert M. Ogden in the Northaven United Methodist Church, Dallas, Texas, March 1969. See also the works mentioned previously in footnote 4 of this chapter.

stantial change or attitudinal change, as in the case of Biafran children, who were not old enough to be capable of adult intentionality of decision, the eternal, unconditional love of God constitutes the Saving Possibility.

Our confidence in the ultimacy of God's love must not in any way reduce our efforts toward the improvement of our neighbor's life and circumstance, as I have already insisted. *Our love for our neighbor,* as I have likewise suggested, *is grounded in God's love and commanded by his love.* This real test of love for God, as superbly drawn out in Matthew's Parable of the Last Judgment (chapter 25), is our meeting the needs of our neighbor. Our confidence in God's love is our reason for meeting our neighbor's needs, but likewise our reason for refusing to place our final hope in either the success or failure of man's best efforts.

To say this is, of course, to reiterate the most basic of Christian theological assertions: in God alone is our final trust for past, present, and future. And precisely because our real life is truly and finally in God alone, we are set free to be our deepest selves for others. God's love is a free gift, but never a cheap gift, and we must not continue to confuse "free" with "cheap." After all, the cross, properly understood, is both a sentence of death and a summons to life.

The Gospel as Life Affirmed
contours of celebration

2

I have suggested the presence of a Saving Possibility in all situations as one way to refocus a main thrust of the gospel. The reality of the Saving Possibility, grounded in God's all-encompassing and unconditional love, calls for a theology of celebration, affirmation, and hope.

So, in this chapter I offer the reader a very unsystematic, yet somewhat comprehensive, sketch of life affirmed vis-à-vis the gospel. These images will call you to confrontation, confession, commitment, and most of all, celebration or affirmation of life. Some of these words have a self-evident meaning which confronts the reader with a decision. Others have a more flexible quality, arousing curiosity and impregnating the imagination. Sometimes the language makes use of Christian categories or vocabulary. On other occasions the language of psychological insight offers an incognito Christian theology. But whoever you are and by whatever name you call yourself, these words point to what it means for human beings *as human beings* to live their lives with a quality of celebration, victory, and hope.

How we can appropriate these visions of affirmation into our lives is, of course, the ongoing struggle of our existence. There is no easy or once-and-for-all "how." We can be certain, however, that these celebrative possibilities constitute the gracious gifts of God which call us to decide who we are and who we will become.

CELEBRATION IS WHEN . . .

you keep rediscovering that life
WILL SUSTAIN YOU
WILL SUSTAIN YOU
WILL SUSTAIN YOU

even when you're <u>dead</u>

certain it's not going to

EASTER
X
G O D
D
U
S

YOUR CONFIDENCE IS IN GOD'S FUTURE
INSTEAD OF YOUR OWN PAST

LIFE'S MEANING IS NOT IN OUR RIGHTNESS
OR ACHIEVEMENTS OF THE PAST

BUT IN OUR FREEDOMFORTHEFUTURE

you become convinced that you can re-
possess your life because God is always giving your life back to you as a brand new
GIFT no matter how you may have

Sold it in hock
lost it
𝔰𝔠𝔯𝔢𝔴𝔢𝔡 𝔦𝔱 𝔲𝔭
defaulted it
asphyxiated it
wounded it
misused it
humiliated it
deadened it
failed it

CELEBRATION IS WHEN . . .

YOU PICK   LIVE
        UP   AND YOUR
        YOUR   LIFE
        PALLET

                IN SPITE OF
                    ALL THE IN SPITE OFS
                    OF LIFE

                        instead of surrendering to a
                        paralyzing victim image
        the only way
        anyone EVER lives his life is in spite of the
                                    in spite ofs

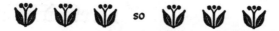

            lift up your heads and rejoice
                for water is made into wine
                winter becomes spring
                death is turned into life
                it is the Lord's doing

                    and it is marvelous in our eyes

you are free to fail because you know it's not the end of the world when you do

what does it mean to trust the gospel? it means that no failure is ultimate it means tomorrow is not dependent on what happened yesterday it means the future comes as God's invitation to become you are forever dying to that which keeps you from

l
i
v
i
n
g

your life
SO THAT

the sentence of death becomes the summons to life

hearing others becomes as important to you
as their hearing you

REMEMBER:

there are few people who will pay $25 or more
to listen to a speech for an hour, even if a
guru is speaking, but there are thousands who
pay $25 or more per hour week after week for
years in order to BE HEARD.

so   *-listen*
         listen
         listen

H-

CELEBRATION IS WHEN . . .

you are free not only _from_ your past, but also free _for_ your past so that the past becomes your

> set of building blocks
> instead of stumbling blocks

we cannot pretend that the past does not exist, nor can we disconnect ourselves from its reality any more than we can jump out of our skin . . . but we can learn to use the past so that its former demons become suppliers of revelatory insight and intuition into human nature,

> and thereby we
> have become stronger because of our
> former weaknesses

these are among our greatest victories of life

CELEBRATION IS WHEN . . .

*you wake up to the danger of becoming a failure in
your successes, and to the grace of becoming a success
in your failures*

*the first shall be last, and the last first
he who exalts himself will be humbled, and the
humbled exalted
every valley shall be lifted up and every mountain
be made low*

CELEBRATION IS WHEN . . .

your LOVE
for the
oppressed
is not an
emotional
hang-up
disguising
HATE
for the
establishment

somehow you can give thanks in (not for) all circumstances

shall we give thanks only when Yahweh's way is our way?

TO CELEBRATE IS TO EUCHARIZE

ou can distinguish between:

neurosis that someone is projecting on you and a prophetic word of truthful criticism directed your way (including those directed by neurotic persons)

it requires all the wisdom and discernment of which you are capable, and then some, to sort out what needs to be sorted out in critical comments which are directed at you. because all people, even very neurotic ones, are capable of seeing and articulating truth. so you may say to yourself, "is this person projecting his perfectionistic tendencies or some other pathological hang-up on me, in which case the problem is essentially *his*, or, am I hearing a word of truth which I *need to hear about myself?*" or maybe there is an element of both. the only way to sort these things out is to KNOW YOURSELF inside out upside down from cover to cover

CELEBRATION IS WHEN . . .

you
keep
rediscovering
    that
    you
    do
    notnotnotnotnotnotnotnotnotnotnotnotnotnot
    have
    to
    live
    your
    life
    as
    though
        you
        were
        on
        trial,
            as
            though
            you
            had
            to
            prove
            yourself
            to
            others
            as
            a
            human
            being

you are grasped by a trinity of LOVE

OR YOURSELF
OR THE OPPRESSED
OR YOUR ENEMIES

This combination is revolutionary, and always comes into the world as a new reality, a rarity among men.

In traditional terms this is the demand and the promise of CHRISTMAS, The Birthday of THE REVOLUTION

CELEBRATION IS WHEN . . .

you celebrate again and again
"a mystery called Grace that
keeps interrupting the tragedy
and despair of our lives with
epiphanies of joy and meaning."

Howard Moody
Judson Memorial Church
Greenwich Village

you can see those
with whom you
are polarized as
HUMAN BEINGS

      you no longer
      have to niggerize
      your opponents by
      stereotyping and
      dehumanizing them

           you no longer
           "write people off"
           because of the color
           of their skin or the
           color of their ideas

what do people with whom you are
polarized look like to you?

do they look like pigs or lefty q. liberals?

do they look like "trees walking"?

or do they look like persons?

66

you quit looking for the wrong certitude
(escape from finitude and freedom) and
grasp the one abiding certitude that was
in the beginning, is now, and ever shall be:

IN EVERY SITUATION
A SAVING POSSIBILITY IS GIVEN

the saving possibility which is given in
every situation may not be the one you
wanted, the one you would have chosen,
the one you were looking for; you may not
perceive it, but its presence does not depend on whether you see it or not, because
THE SAVING POSSIBILITY IS THERE.

you know that what makes life HOLY

is

THE WHOLE

life, thank God, is not just you, or even you and all your experiences and relationships. but more than that. life is not just the sum total of all creatures and their relationships and experiences. THE WHOLE is more . . . THE WHOLE includes the transcendent reality

of the givenness of all that is
of the future which comes to us
of the claim upon us to live and love
of the passing away of all that is—

EXCEPT
THE
WHOLE

CELEBRATION IS WHEN . . .

you re-cog-nize the gift of your vul
                              ner
                                 ability

                                        is at times

             the greatest gift you can offer to o
                                                  t
                                                   h
                                                    e
                                                     r
                                                      s

while at other times it is the gift of confrontation

you see that God is PERSON-al--not because he removes the difficulty of decision-making and personal responsibility not because he somehow makes things come out the way we hope they will (what kind of "person" would that be?) but because he gives us himself in terms of our future and because in all situations a free rebirth is given without which we could not become persons

CELEBRATION IS WHEN . . .

YOU discover that those with whom we relate need both ACCEPTANCE and EXPECTATION from us, as we do from them

without expectation a relationship is a neurotic conspiracy by which those involved agree to deal with each other as less than adult human beings

without acceptance a relationship is characterized by legalistic lovelessness and suffocating self-righteousness

YOUr
e
w
a
r
d

f
o
r

caring about others

IS

caring about others

you realize that the greatest possible WISH which a human being could wish has already been given and fulfilled

you receive the
YESwhichis
ineveryNO "yes" of
life

you come to the conclusion that

LIFE AFTER BIRTH

and

LIFE BEFORE DEATH

are more important than

LIFE AFTER DEATH

you   affirm
        that the strong
    (whoever they are)

        need the weak
    (whoever they are)

as much as
    the   weak
        need the
            strong

CELEBRATION IS WHEN . . .

you accept your life as g-o-o-d AS GIVEN

After all, Jesus' authority among men was not an unusual I.Q., a mystical otherworldliness, or a winsome personality. Nor was it economic, social, or political power. In part, at least, his authority was his freedom to receive his life as being good as given

it was good that his parents were who they were; that his life was in the time of history it was in; that he was a male Jew; it was good to be a carpenter, to associate with all kinds of people, to receive the gifts which life offered; all of it was good.

your life is good, too

you begin to
live in the what IS world rather than the what-
COULD-HAVE-BEEN world or the what-
MIGHT-BE world

in other words, the IS world, not the IF world

Note: While we live in the IS world, we must
also be at work in the what-MIGHT-BE
world . . . a world of justice and freedom.

you declare peace with life by accepting the terms upon which life is offered

NAMELY

U R LIMITED

Surrender to God is not surrender of your selfhood, your freedom, your responsibility. Surrender to God is accepting the terms by which life is offered. Then you can begin the celebration of life as it actually is (in all of its limitedness)

CELEBRATION IS WHEN . . .

Y
O
U

T
A
K
E

C
H
A
R
G
E

O
F

YOUR
L
I
F
E

and put to rest the lie
that someone else
can live your life for you

CELEBRATION IS WHEN . . .

you accept the fact that there's only ONE WAY out of Egypt:

AND THAT'S THROUGH THE WILDERNESS

Once we've experienced an exodus, an event of newfound freedom, we are inevitably confronted with the decision: Back to Egypt? or On to Canaan through the wilderness?

For the way of the wilderness is the way of the unknown and the unmapped. At least with Pharaoh in Egypt there was routine, familiarity, predictability, and security, even if it was second-class citizenship. Hear the murmurings? "For God's sake, Moses, what have you gotten us into? We're hungry, thirsty, tired, and there are warlike people over the next hill! We were better off in Egypt!"

No matter how much we've hoped and longed for a newfound freedom, and no matter how good it is to us, there is something in us which beckons us to go back to the safety of bondage in Egypt.

For Exodus is always toward maturity, risk, discovery of self, responsible use of freedom. And the only way out of Egypt is through the wilderness. In the wilderness we have only one thing going for us, and that is GOD'S PROMISE that he will sustain us and lead us and guide us with manna from heaven, water from the rock, and a vision (decalogue) of the way. In the wilderness God's Promise is our only guarantee. When we learn again and again to rely on that promise, a strange thing happens.
THE WILDERNESS
ISN'T THE WILDERNESS
ANYMORE. THE WILDERNESS
HAS BECOME

THE PROMISED LAND.

you
discover
the
greatest
mystery
and
wonder
of all is

ISNESS

Your prayer is your willingness to receive whatever may come as a sign of God's all-embracing love (instead of a technique to "get God into the situation") the longer I live the more I'm convinced that to know God's will is not so much to know the whys and wherefores of what happens but to receive all circumstances as gift-bearing possibilities

IN THE MIDST of your hurt feelings, you can realize that for every time someone hurts you, you have hurt someone else; that for every time others have been insensitive to you, you have been so to them. The demonic nature of hurt feelings is that we see ourselves only as the injured, but not as those who have injured others. That's why we have prayers of confession. They hold our noses up against our tendency to nourish our hurt feelings more than we cultivate a sense of maturity.

ARISE
N
D

COME FORTH
LAZARUS, BABY!

CELEBRATION IS WHEN . . .

COMMUNITY
becomes more important than
COMMODITIES

PERSONS
become more precious than
PLASTICS
PROPERTY
PROFITS

HANG   **AND**   **ON**
    LOOSE   **TURN**

CELEBRATION IS WHEN . . .

> **"you are a perfectly free lord of all,
> subject to NONE
> you are a perfectly dutiful servant of all,
> subject to ALL"**

**M. Luther
Priest, Prophet, Reformer,
  and Celebrator of Life
    who shared in Christ's
      kingship and priesthood
        and called us to do likewise**

      **lord of all
      servant of all
        Combine these two and live!**

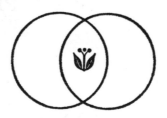

you begin to find the real, the ultimate, the true not in the thought of
lemonade on the front porch and 18
holes every day in some future existence,

b
u
t

in the HELL of the world—

the hurts
the wounds
the humiliations
the needs

OF

thehungrythedispossessed
theoutcaststheleastofthese

you experience the metamorphosis of

DO UNTO OTHERS AS THEY
DO UNTO YOU DO UNTO
OTHERS AS YOU WOULD HAVE
THEM DO UNTO YOU DO UNTO
OTHERS AS christ HAS DONE
UNTO YOU

you realize that the

is ONE WORD

all is G iven
all is R eceived
all is A ccepted
all is C onfirmed
all is E mbraced

CELEBRATION IS WHEN . . .

ON THE ONE HAND

you finally decide that no one can solve your problems FOR you

not the right person
not the right group
not the right relationship
not the right dogma
not the right activity
not the right political party
not the right church
not the right therapist
not the right guru
not even Jesus

Jesus never solved anyone's problem FOR him. he was the catalytic change agent who pointed to the gifts of God waiting to be unleashed and liberated, already present in the people of God. that's all anyone can do "for" you. others can bear your burdens with you, but not for you. you must decide where you want to go with your life, and who you want to be becoming. no one can solve your problems for you but you.

ON THE OTHER HAND

you cannot solve your problems apart from your neighbor. but your choice need not be between entombed independence and parasitical dependence. your possibility is in interdependence, in community which enables you to bring about desired changes. no one ever becomes who he can become apart from community.

by the same token you cannot solve other people's problems *for* them. you cannot live anyone else's life for him. you can only be a good neighbor—one who helps point to God's gifts already present—one who offers encouragement and concern—one who bears with but not for.

but, someone will say, did not Jesus die FOR us? Is not this page a mistake? even if we say Jesus died for us, it still doesn't solve our problems for us. we must *decide* again and again to appropriate his death as a claim on us for renewed living.

CELEBRATION IS WHEN . . .
you use the time of your life
to encourage the discouraged
to lift up the downtrodden
to insist on dignity and justice for all

not because you'll get a sugar-coated reward
down the road
not because you can obligate the recipients of
your service
not because it's good for your reputation in the
community
not because you can get people to accept you if
you sacrifice for them
not because it's a character-building thing to do
not because you can then justify getting away
with inhumanity in other ways
not because you can boast that you are a
righteous person

(although these reasons are frequently part of our motivations)

but because that is what life is for in the first place

you move beyond the notion, so often taught in the church, and in very religious homes, that it is wrong to love yourself

love what God loves

and not only that - if you detest yourself, you won't really affirm your neighbor . . . because the way you feel about yourself is the way you will project toward others . . .

FromFromm: self love is the opposite of self-ishness
FromtheGospel: the basis of authentic self-love is
God's
unconditional, everlasting love
for all men

CELEBRATION IS WHEN . . .

you communicate to your children that it is
GOOD to become an adult

chronologically
emotionally
physically
MENTALLY
sexually
𝔯𝔢𝔩𝔦𝔤𝔦𝔬𝔲𝔰𝔩𝔶

and in every other way

whether you are a man or a woman . . .
You know—I mean REALLY know
                    that women are PERSONS

not merely extensions or appendages or helpmates
of their husbands

masculinity does not depend on second-class citizenship for women
femininity does not depend on the mystique of biological destiny

YOU

begin

to

prefer

reality

to

ILLusion

you accept the fact that no matter how threatening change may appear, the reality of change is the unconditional prerequisite for life to have meaning

NO CHANGE=NO LIFE=NONBEING

YOU
BECOME
AS
CONCERNED
ABOUT
YOUR
ECOLOGICAL
STANDARD
OF
LIVING
AS
YOUR
ECONOMIC
STANDARD
OF
LIVING;
WHEN
YOU
RELATE
TO
NATURE
AS
THOUGH
IT
WERE
A
COMMUNITY
RATHER
THAN
A
COMMODITY

WONDER INVADES
YOUR BEING
AND MAKES
YOU A CHILD
AGAIN

(for shannon and john)

you decide to
live for a truth in which the
only ASSURANCE OF VIC-
TORY IS THE VICTORY OF
LIVING FOR THAT TRUTH

like the Gospel

The Gospel as Persons Affirmed
the pastorhood of all believers

3

In chapter 1 we focused on the Christian gospel as the good news of a Saving Possibility in all situations. In this chapter, I will suggest what this gospel "looks like" when applied to supportive forms of congregational care and concern, both in normal times and in the midst of trials and tribulations. The latter might include surgery, terminal illness, loss of relationship, the facing of extremely difficult decisions, and personal frustrations or failures. We will consider an emerging emphasis on pastoral care by laymen, destructive and constructive attempts to offer concern and support for others, two basic assumptions related to this concern and support, and some methods for sensitizing and developing the ministry of lay pastoral care. Hopefully, this chapter will challenge pastors and laymen alike to work together for a mutually shared pastorhood of all believers.

An Emerging Emphasis

In the past twenty years, a growing emphasis on the recovery or renaissance of the laity has gained widespread attention in the church. This ministry of the laity movement is now bringing about a renewed emphasis on the ministering church, so that pastoral care is increasingly seen as the province of the laity as well as the clergy. Thus, the ministry of the laity concept is beginning to be integrated with the pastoral care concept, resulting in a pastoral care which is the shared function of the whole church.

When one considers the thrust of New Testament images of the church, even a cursory glance reveals that the ministry of care and reconciliation is entrusted to the whole church, not just to a set-apart, ordained person. The images of the church as the People of God in mission, the Servant of God, the New Humanity, a Community of Believers, all suggest a corporate ministry. In addition, they suggest that the role of the clergyman or ordained pastor is that of training his people for their rightful ministry to others. In this role of equipping God's people for their ministry of service (Ephesians 4:11-12), the clergyman is, as H. Richard Niebuhr expressed it, "a teacher of teachers, a counselor of counselors, a pastor of pastors." [1] The involvement of laymen in pastoral care is thoroughly biblical, and is certainly germane to the principles of the Protestant Reformation. In the performance of the pastoral care ministry, the laity becomes the church in action and not merely on paper.

One of the most significant articulations of the implications for the layman of the church's ministry of pastoral care has come from C. W. Brister in his

[1] *The Purpose of the Church and Its Ministry* (New York: Harper & Row, 1956), pp. 83 ff.

book *Pastoral Care in the Church*. In his introduction he says:

Protestant pastoral care views the Church itself as minister, and the pastor as a servant of servants. His role as leader, teacher, and example is fulfilled within the Church's shepherding ministry. God's people care for hurt humanity as they incarnate his redemptive presence in life, where the real needs are. (John 17:15-26) The Church thus finds its life in the world by grappling with the evils, distress, and unanswered questions of men "for Christ's sake." [2]

Not only can we point to a biblical emphasis on the priesthood and pastorhood of all believers, but to pragmatic reasons as well. No matter how alert, wise, well-trained, and supportive the ordained representative of the faith community may be, he is only one person and is bounded by limitations of time, energy, and ability. Of at least equal significance are the capacities of laymen for supportive relationships due to their own gifts, experiences, and numerical strength. By sheer mathematics, laymen outnumber clergymen approximately three hundred to one.[3] Laymen have contacts, "coffee cup" relationships, and open access to many people who either do not know a clergyman or who would be hesitant to see one.

Why, then, since there are both biblical and

[2] (New York: Harper & Row, 1964), Introduction, pp. xxiii-xxiv. Also, see chapter 4, "The Pastoral Action of the Church."

[3] Howard J. Clinebell, Jr., *Mental Health Through Christian Community* (Nashville: Abingdon Press, 1965), p. 261.

practical reasons undergirding lay pastoral care, has the church been so slow and hesitant to move with stronger insistence in this direction? Without detailing a reply, the following assertions at least provide some clues: 1) Many pastors are ill trained themselves for pastoral care and are unable to give much aid in training others. 2) Some pastors will not delegate or share their ministry of pastoral care, due to their own insecurity or their fear that laymen will not be able to handle the complexities of grief and distress with which they are likely to be confronted in pastoral ministry. 3) Many laymen are unwilling to commit themselves to the kind of training necessary to be competent in sustained pastoral care, and they are accustomed to the clergymen shouldering these responsibilities.

Even most of the contemporary writers and educators in the field of pastoral care have only recently begun to take more seriously the congregational dimension of pastoral care. Sometimes, though it is acknowledged that pastoral care is a shared responsibility of the whole church, the assumption remains that lay ministry is one of helping the pastor to fulfill his responsibility. Writers like Howard Clinebell and Seward Hiltner have offered helpful insights into lay pastoral care, but it still remains on the periphery of pastoral ministry.[4] My purpose is not

[4] Examples are Clinebell's chapter 16, "The Layman's Ministry of Pastoral Care and Counseling," from *Basic Types of Pastoral Counseling* (Nashville: Abingdon Press, 1966); Hiltner's section on "The Layman as Pastoral Theologian," from his chapter 2 in *Preface to Pastoral Theology* (Nashville: Abingdon Press, 1958); William Hulme's reference to the pastorhood of the believer in *Pastoral Care Come of Age* (Nashville: Abingdon Press, 1970), p. 89.

to criticize authors for a task they did not intend to include within their scope, but rather to suggest the relative dearth of published material related to pastoral care vis-à-vis the congregation.

In spite of biblical and pragmatic reasons to the contrary, there have been at least two valid reasons why leaders in the field of pastoral care have been somewhat hesitant to endorse too quickly the advance of lay pastoral care. One is that clinical pastoral education, largely geared for ordained clergymen, has had to fight for its own right to thrive as a component of the clergyman's education. Understandably, considerable effort has been expended by pastoral care educators to nourish and strengthen this trend, since most training of laymen would have to depend anyway on trained clergymen and concerned pastors.

The second reason for caution is, as Hiltner and Brister et al have made clear, that the desire by laymen to help needs to be matched with training and informal understanding. Integrity in pastoral work presupposes at least a certain degree of theological and clinical wisdom, to say nothing of reasonable clarity of self-understanding. The point is *not* that laymen have less ability or gifts than clergymen. The point *is* that there are some levels or dimensions of pastoral care which *no one* is likely to perform very well without adequate training, experience, and supervision.

With these considerations in mind, I believe we can say that there is today a slowly emerging emphasis in the significance of pastoral care as a shared task and ministry. Later in the chapter, I will offer some examples of sensitizing and training for the ministry of lay pastoral care. First, however, I want to outline some destructive and constructive ways in which we can offer a supportive ministry to others, both in normal and in stress situations.

In spite of the emerging emphasis I've pointed out, the vast majority of laymen in our churches will *not* be involved in virtually any form of clinical pastoral education for laymen. Possibly these outlines of destructive and constructive means of relating to others will be of some assistance, especially to those who are not to be involved in formal training. Even without systematic or formal training, persons can increase their skills of sensitive care if they are aware of some basic dynamics of human relationships. We can realistically hope that our preaching, personal contacts, and the adult education within the church have an instructive and constructive influence on the ability of at least some church members to more faithfully render a ministry of pastoral care.

Destructive Attempts to Be Supportive

Most pastors have been in situations again and again where well-meaning friends and neighbors have attempted to be of help to those experiencing sorrowful or troubled times. Frequently we see or hear things which we think are more destructive than constructive, in spite of the good intentions involved. As clergymen, we too are frequently trapped by unquestioned assumptions of our own, or by the sheer uncertainty so often present in grief or crisis situations. And sometimes there is no doubt that laymen are more understanding and helpful to people in need than those of us who are clergymen. Following are three illustrations of often used approaches to people which I believe are essentially destructive, whether offered by clergy or by laity.

1. *Destructive theologizing.* How often I have heard well-meaning clergymen and laymen say to a person who has experienced the loss of a loved one, "It was the will of God." If we mean to say that in terms of grace and suffering-love, God is just as fully in the no's of life as well as the yes's, then why not say it that way? If we intend to communicate that all is received, embraced, and affirmed by God, then let us indicate so in some such words. If we mean that in spite of the event that has brought sorrow and confusion, we can still live our lives, then let us indicate our affirmation in appropriate language.

When we attribute unexpected death or other forms of separation to the "will of God," we are teaching children that God is a tyrant to be despised or feared. We are stiffarming adults with a "theological put-down," sealing off real feelings of guilt, anger, and frustration, and encouraging repression of these real feeling needs. And we are denying the gospel by presupposing that God is the direct cause of suffering, rather than the meaning or Saving Possibility giver in the midst of suffering encountered in a world of human freedom and finitude.

People use "the will of God" approach because

they don't know what else to say, and because they think it will offer comfort. It can also be a way of protecting ourselves from the real feelings of those who have suffered loss. After all, who among us will openly argue with the very will of God, especially with friends who are trying to console us? Unquestionably we do encounter people who seem to be comforted by the "it was God's will" approach. We should not foreclose the possibility that some people, because of their background, may actually be sustained by theological assertions not acceptable or helpful to others. Whether or not this kind of theology can enable a person to really face grief instead of avoiding it, however, seems to me to remain a significant question.

Many times we do better to be silent than to traffic in destructive theology, well-intentioned though it may be. Our personal presence itself is usually its own "word," and may mean much more than theological "overkill." In *The Dynamics of Grief,* David Switzer quotes Jeshaia Schnitzer as saying that, even though "friends may have nothing to say, their very presence with the bereaved when he feels that the world is empty and void, has its remedial effects." [5] The language of relationship can itself be a sign of concern reflecting God's unconditional love which brings Saving Possibilities in all situations. As Reuel L. Howe put it, "The Gospel is a saving event that occurs in human relations

[5] (Nashville: Abingdon Press, 1970), p. 202. He quotes from Jeshaia Schnitzer, "Thoughts on Bereavement and Grief," *Reconstructionist* (1955), CXXXI: 120.

and is not a body of knowledge for mere verbal transmission." [6]

2. *Sympathetic overreaction.* A member of the congregation that I presently serve told me of an experience while she was in the hospital. Prior to major surgery which she was to undergo, the hospital chaplain came by for a visit and offered a prayer. His prayer, in the opinion of my friend, seemed more suited to meet the needs of the chaplain in the situation, than in meeting her needs as she faced the prospects of surgery. My intent here is not to blame the chaplain, if indeed any blame is appropriate or needed. My purpose is to call our attention to an elusive but important aspect in relating to people in stress situations: are we projecting our own feelings in a damaging way onto the other person whose burden we are attempting to share?

At times the comforter and the comforted may both outwardly express their emotions by embracing, crying, or whatever is meaningful. This can be redemptive and reassuring. However, sometimes well-intentioned people fall into a maudlin sympathy which reinforces a sense of helplessness on those who have suffered a loss. This incarnation of gloom and doom on the part of those who would comfort others communicates hopelessness and complicates the picture rather than being a source of renewing comfort. Whether we are clergymen or laymen, we need to cultivate all the self-awareness which is pos-

[6] *The Miracle of Dialogue* (New York: The Seabury Press, 1965), p. 149.

sible in order to be aware of what and how we are communicating to others.

3. *Advice giving from on high.* All of us have innate tendencies to control what is going on around us, including the decisions of other people. Particularly in grief situations, whether it be a person facing a divorce, loss of a job, alienation of a relationship, or a grief related to death, our controlling instincts often shift into high gear. Phrases like, "If I were you," or "Don't you think you ought to . . ." are representative of an assumption that somehow, whether by divine revelation or native wizardry, we know best for the lives of other people. These are, of course, very questionable presuppositions for which there are no substantial arguments.

I recall one situation in which a young wife with two small children had experienced the death of her husband. Within two weeks of his death she received the following advice from friends who somehow assumed that they knew more about what she should do than she herself knew:

"If I were you I'd get back to work as quickly as you can. That way you'll be busy and get this off your mind as much as possible."

"Don't you think you should take some time off and not get back to work too soon? Give yourself a rest and take a vacation."

"I'm sure you've already thought about selling the house. I know it must be tough to be here with so many associations of your husband."

"I kind of hope you'll stay here. You have so many wonderful associations of your husband here.

109

I know it would be difficult to leave those behind and have someone else living here."

Is it any wonder, after conflicting advice from "expert" friends and relatives, that a person would feel more confused and paralyzed? As would-be comforters and friends, we would do well to remember that (a) we probably do not know what is best for someone else, especially if we've never experienced what they are experiencing; (b) we probably don't know what is best for someone else even if we have been down a similar road of experience, because they are who *they* are, and we are who *we* are. We cannot assume that they will, or should, respond the same way that we did on either the feeling or the action level; (c) even if by some magic we did know what might be best for someone else, it is antithetical to a supporting and caring ministry to allow ourselves to be peddlers of advice. It seldom helps people to grow and mature and trust in their own decisions when others try to decide for them, even in a subtle way.

Our presence and our concern may be facilitators for searching and decision-making for persons who are facing a new future or a difficult time. Our support is not in the form of making decisions for them, but in the form of personal respect, support, and concern, so that they can make their own decisions. Sometimes, when technical advice is sought, we can be of help according to our expertise in that field of knowledge. For example: an insurance man helps a widow understand her options on a policy; a lawyer explains possibilities under a trust agreement or social security arrangement; or, at the invitation of the grieving person, a close friend explores options and decisions of various kinds when the time is right, as indicated by the bereaved.

If my own experiences and observations in the ministry are accurate gauges, I would say that there is too much well-intentioned giving of the tongue and not enough giving of the ear, the heart, and the hand. If our advice is unheeded, we've wasted our breath. If our advice is poor, we are to blame for our bad directions and will be separated to that extent from our friend. And even if our advice appears sound by subsequent action, we have not necessarily helped our friend to grow and mature as a person or to be better equipped for the next problem with which he must deal. Certainly there can be good advice at times, but I have to say I've heard more of a doubtful quality than of genuine help.

Constructive Attempts to Be Supportive

In this section I will indicate three general suggestions which I believe can be constructive ways of enabling people in grief or troubled circumstances to maximize their own potentials. These will be "in season" in virtually any situation, and are basic to Christian pastoral care, whether clerical or lay. It should be obvious that these are not substitutes for professional training and insights into matters that are frequently highly complex. However, these three suggestions have proven themselves again and again in my own ministry, and I commend them as basic foundations to clergy and laity alike.

One of our most creative ways of helping people is to accept their feelings. As a pastor concerned with my ability to relate meaningfully to others, and equally concerned with empowering laymen to minister to each other, there is no assertion more essential than this. If we can try to understand how a person feels, and receive whatever those feelings are, we are involved in a life-giving and receiving relationship. If we can accept negative and hostile feelings which are expressed, we are affirming some of the deepest needs of that person, and entering into the hidden layers of his world. In so doing, we help that person to accept himself and to move toward a new and creative future.

How do we respond when, in being with a person who has suffered a traumatic separation, he or she says something like, "I feel as though God has let me down"? Do we jump to God's defense, and become the articulate theologian? Do we assure the person that God is good and they have no right to feel or think that way, especially when so many other people are less fortunate? Or do we receive these negative feelings as perfectly understandable, or, at least, as the *real* feelings of that person, whether such feelings are understandable or not? If we respond with something like, "You know, it does seem like God lets us down sometimes," we are saying to that person that it is all right to feel that way; that they are accepted with all of their doubts and frustrations; that they can trust us and themselves with their feelings; that they are affirmed as human beings.

If this example can be used as symbolic of a way to relate to people, we will be offering to people the kind of loving and affirming acceptance reflected in the Christian gospel. Traditional forms of verbalizing the gospel, as well as more contemporary expressions, have profound implications on the way we relate to other persons. "While we were yet sinners, Christ died for the *un*godly." That statement presupposes a theology of acceptance, and constitutes a basic premise for clerical and lay pastoral care. It means that if we are to bear with other persons in times of their need, we need to be open to the whole person as he is. To be open to the real person as he is is to bear witness in relational terms to the unconditional, all-embracing love of God, and the Saving Possibility inherent in that all-encompassing love.

The ministry of nonjudgmental listening is a form of participating presence which says, "You are not alone as you face this situation . . . there are those who try to understand, and who affirm you as a human being . . . we are not afraid of your world, including your real feelings . . . we think the innate capacity to move through this valley is within you, and that what our presence may offer is to help that capacity be fulfilled and realized."

Listening for feelings and intent, and not just for content, is an essential characteristic of a helping relationship. Active listening, as it is sometimes called by psychologists, psychiatrists, and other counselors, requires the listener to put himself in the shoes of the sender of the message. As we prepare to accept another in his distress, his frustration, and his doubt, we can hope to enter into his world, seeing and sensing that world as he feels it and experiences it. We cannot do this if we assume that the answer is in ourselves instead of in the other person.

Philip Anderson has put it in these words:

. . . we are listening not only for the objective discussion, but also for the very sake and being of the other person. We listen without judgment or criticism or superiority, but with love. We try hard to understand the world from the point of view of the speaker. We put ourselves in the shoes of the other person. Such listening with an open heart and mind *feels* the grief, the loneliness, the despair, the hurt, the doubts of that person. When there is this kind of listening, a person may reveal secrets that have been a source of anxiety and a lonely burden for years. He knows that he is at one with his hearer, that there is no need to keep up pretenses. He can speak honestly, knowing that he will be understood and accepted.[7]

Although we can never accept another human being unconditionally, we can help the latent inner resources of an individual come to fuller and freer expression through a relationship based on acceptance of feelings. As Hiltner and many others have pointed out, acceptance does not necessarily mean agreement; it means affirmation of the worth of that human being, whatever his feelings might be, and his right to have those feelings. When this ac-

[7] *Church Meetings That Matter* (Philadelphia: United Church Press, 1965), pp. 29-30.

ceptance occurs, it offers our neighbor the re-presentation of both God's love and the resulting renewed possibility of himself being a neighbor to others in need.

A second suggestion for offering supportive relationships comes from the passage in the fourth chapter of the letter to the Ephesians. The author exhorts us to *speak the truth in love.* (vs. 15) Generally speaking, the vast majority of people can bear a great deal of hard-to-hear reality when they are informed and dealt with in a forthright but concerned way. In quite a few situations I have found that people are actually grateful and relieved to find someone who will not be evasive but who will converse realistically in a concerned way about the problem at hand.

A common tendency is to overshield a person who is facing, or who has faced, a particular dilemma. The result is that he is isolated in his problem and is forced into playing the "we-all-know-what's-going-on-here-but-we're-not-going-to-talk-about-it" game.[8] A feeling of release can be experienced in a relationship in which there is no reliance on phony saving possibilities, evasion of reality, and the use of euphemistic jargon ("passed away"), but instead an honest facing of the situation at hand in a loving and honest way.

I am not suggesting that we all take it upon ourselves to be the unabashed revealers of everything we know or suspect. Nor am I suggesting that we

---

[8] Those who have read Tolstoy's *The Death of Ivan Ilych* will recall the classic refusal of Ilych's family and friends to talk with him about his dying and suffering.

have no regard for the apparent capacity for truth on the part of our friends. My own observations, however, lead me to believe that we are much more likely to err in the direction of being evasive in the face of hard facts. The plain truth is that we are more comfortable talking about the weather and the latest football score than in openly giving and receiving in a conversation that may be terribly important to a friend facing a difficult situation.

To speak the truth in love is, within our own limits, to be willing to share the grief, the fright, and the other feelings of those with whom we seek to offer a supportive relationship. To speak the truth in love is to refuse to play phony games of escape when a friend indicates that he wants to talk about his predicament. To speak the truth in love is to be realistic and honest, offering to our neighbor the courage to face what needs to be faced. It is this courage which is so all-important in perceiving and appropriating a Saving Possibility in times of difficult choices.

A third major supportive direction of the concerned person is to communicate the reality that *no situation is hopeless.* Our privilege as the community of Christ is to communicate by who we are and what we do that there is a Saving Possibility in every situation, as asserted in Chapter 1. We are the incurable hopers, the harbingers of hope, called to bring good tidings to the afflicted, and to bind up the brokenhearted. We can do this because our ultimate confidence is in God, who is always bringing a Saving Possibility into life even if it may not be the one we would have chosen. That's who God is, and that's what God does.

How can we communicate a healthy and undying hope about the outcome of a dark night, a hopefulness that is not a substitute for the real grieving process, but rather a hope which embraces good grief and good struggle? Sometimes we do so through a searching glance and/or the press of a hand. In the past couple of years, more and more pastors have been deeply impressed by the power of touch when it seems appropriate as a sign of concern. The early Christians utilized the laying on of hands and the kiss of peace. These have been jokingly referred to and put aside in many sophisticated middle-class congregations; that is, until the human potential movement of our day reopened our eyes to its resources.

In my early ministry I avoided the use of touch, for the most part. Now I am convinced that this was an over-reaction to my image of some ministers as back-slappers, baby-kissers, and artificial huggers. My own growth as a human being has convinced me that either the touch of a hand across a hospital bed or a gentle embrace at the right time can be a vehicle of hope and concern when used in good taste by ministers and laymen who are comfortable in so doing. Those who are ill and who are experiencing heretofore unexperienced feelings are likely to feel cut off, isolated, or rejected. Touch symbolizes acceptance and union with life and community. As Edwin M. McMahon and Peter A. Campbell remind us in their remarkable use of words and pictures

117

in *Please Touch,* touch can involve wonder, reaching out, knowing, growing, and loving.[9]

Without being naïve about the potential risks of touch, I must say that I have seen the use of touch in verbal and nonverbal encounter groups literally transform the level of trust in more than one group of churchmen. We now begin our church year in the Northaven congregation in September with a twenty-four-hour retreat for our leaders and chairmen in order to put them "in touch" with each other as human beings, utilizing several hours of sensitivity training by a psychiatric social worker. The impressive fact about his approach is that the possible risks are recognized, and no more is claimed for the process than ought to be claimed. The legitimate and genuine contribution of many movements today is diminished by their tendency to claim more for themselves than they ought to claim. But thoughtfully utilized, encounter with touch included can free people to relate to each other on a more deeply personal basis, not only within that group at the time, but in our one-to-one relationships which follow.

As pastors, we have been slow to recognize that we need to minister not only on the level of theological and ecclesiological understanding, but also on the level of feelings and emotions. The discovery of these needs widens our concept of the whole person and the ministry needed to reach out to that person. People can work together for years in an institution and be out of touch with each other as persons.

[9] (New York: Sheed & Ward, 1969).

On the other hand, the Christian community has the tools to meet the basic needs of persons, described by William Glasser as the need to love and be loved (to be close to at least one other person), and the need for self-esteem (to feel worthwhile to oneself and to others).[10]

Along with touch, a simple verbalizing of "we love you" can likewise offer hope. Do we realize how many people virtually never hear those words? Many are those who rarely hear it in their own family circles, much less from some other source. Although the word "love" has been eroded by cultural usage in many ways, it can still convey the message of ultimate hopefulness about life. We of the Body of Christ should not bandy it about carelessly, but neither should we lock it up in the cold storage of intellectual sophistication. I think of one man who was affirmed by a small group within his congregation during a trying time of his life. His response: "I've never had anyone, other than my wife, say to me that I was loved." A community which bears this word of love to its members is offering a powerful antidote for loneliness and loss of identity, especially to those facing fractured relationships and uncertain futures.

The message of hope can also come across by doing very earthy chores for those who may be unable to do them for themselves for the time being. Before doing anything we might ask ourselves, "What can this person do for himself, and what

---

[10] These two basic human needs, other than on the biological level, are suggested by William Glasser in *Reality Therapy* (New York: Harper & Row, 1965).

needs to be done in his behalf at this time?" We may not know the answer, but our aim is to do what needs to be done, but only so as to enable the individual to assume as much responsibility as he can as he is ready. In other words, our aim is not to make others dependent on us, but to free them for normal acceptance of responsibility as they are able to do so.

Another question we need to debate with ourselves is whether or not to go ahead and act, or to ask, "What can I do?" or else to say, "Let me know if I can do anything." The latter may be offered as a communication of availability, but it also sounds like the well-known phrase, "Come and see us sometime." Most people are reticent to ask for help, and thus sometimes it is wise to go ahead and act.

Several years ago, when I was in the hospital with mononucleosis, a friend came to the house and mowed the yard at his own initiative. If he had said to me, "I'd be glad to cut your yard until you can take care of it," I'm quite sure that I would have said, "Oh, that's all right; it's already taken care of." Our decision can be based on how well we know the individual, and how much help they have, as far as we know. On many occasions I have seen women bringing food, or shopping for a family, or taking care of their laundry in times of crisis.

In other circumstances, I remember how a member of the church spent one afternoon per week with the children of a neighboring family where the father-husband had unexpectedly died. This kind of practical concern is the pastorhood of all believers at its best, and represents a highly constructive and supportive help in time of need. Through concern of this kind, the theology of a Saving Possibility becomes real and personal.

Another form of care too often taken for granted is the ministry of mail. If, of course, it becomes an impersonal substitute for a personal ministry, it becomes a liability more than an asset. But it can also supplement our personal presence. We tend to forget how important mail is to the bedridden and the convalescent. In some illnesses the mail becomes a very important contact with the "outside world." Cards and notes let the patient know that he is not forgotten, in spite of the fact that he is out of circulation.

This communication of care is not insignificant to the health and self-esteem of the sick person. Suffering is more bearable, and hope is more promising when community, care, and concern come to us, even in the form of a humorous card from a friend. When even one person cares, that care can say in effect, "This is the kind of world where care is a reality. Because you are cared about, you too can care."

Some of these constructive ways of supporting people were articulated to me recently by a member of the congregation. She spoke of three relationships which were particularly sustaining following the untimely death of her husband. One relationship was with a friend who, over a long period of time, was a nonjudgmental sharer of the grief process. By communicating the fact that the loss was also a hurt to herself, the friend was able to say that she took with utter seriousness and feeling the reality of the grief.

Her second relationship that offered hope was with the surgeon who had been involved in the unsuccessful attempt to save her husband's life. He was someone, as she put it, "whom I could call when I was terribly depressed, when I felt like committing suicide." Through his openness and acceptance of her feelings, she was able, as the doctor himself put it, "to open the door and become acquainted with those feelings instead of shutting them out." She became convinced that a person has got to let it hurt enough to allow it to dissipate over a long period of time. By the acceptance of feelings and by speaking the truth out of a true personal concern, the surgeon was also a priest to his neighbor.

The third relationship began almost a year following her husband's death when she began participating in our congregation. For her, real support occurred through honesty in theological questions offered through preaching and through personal visits. This reality-oriented theology confirmed convictions and feelings she had held for years. As she put it, her old theology was not real, and needed to give way to a more honest and forthright content. These three supporting relationships combined acceptance of feelings, speaking the truth in love, and the holding forth of hope for the future.

Two Basic Assumptions in Lay Pastoral Care

C. W. Brister defines pastoral care as "the mutual concern of Christians for each other and for those in the world for whom Christ died." [11] Elsewhere pastoral care has been defined as support and assistance offered by members of a congregation in both normal and critical times so that the recipients are set free to be themselves and to minister to others. Two verses from a paragraph in Galatians provide us with a necessary balance or creative tension as we seek to give expression to mutual concern through supportive relationships and acts.

On the one hand, Paul says in verse two of the sixth chapter, "Bear one another's burdens, and so fulfill the law of Christ." In verse five of the same paragraph he says that each man will have to bear his own load. The New English Bible translates this, "Everyone has his own proper burden to bear." Actually, Paul uses two different words in these passages for the term "burden." In verse two, he is saying that Christians are bound together in Christ in serving each other, caring about one another, and sharing one another's burdens. In verse five he is suggesting that the oneness of community responsibility does not eliminate the responsibility of each individual to do his share and, so to speak, give his own unique gift of love and service within the community.

What I propose is not to use these passages as a precise interpretive source but as a resource for understanding pastoral care, whether clergy, laity, or both, in a way I believe to be consistent with biblical insight into God and man. When these two passages are merged into a creative balance, they enable us

[11] *Pastoral Care in the Church*, p. xxiii.

to develop realistic expectations of ourselves and of others, and to increase our effectiveness in helping others. They can help guard against the dangers of what I call *"over-bearing"* and *"under-bearing."*

The wise blending of these two passages reminds us that no one can solve someone else's problems *for* him. This is one of the two basic assumptions of pastoral care, lay or otherwise, which I'm emphasizing in this section. If we believe this, we will be more likely to avoid "over-bearing." Here I am speaking of burdens or problems in the sense of the inner self and its weakness and strength. I am not thinking, say, of a scientific problem in which a person with a certain expertise can solve my problem apart from my own effort.

For example, if my car radiator hose breaks, a mechanic or someone who knows how to fix it can solve my problem for me as I stand by, more or less uninvolved. But if we are speaking of the self and its potential, we can be sure that neither the right person, group, relationship, activity, doctrine, church, therapist, or the right anything else, will solve our problems *for* us. The problem of the self and the potential of the self are rooted within the self, and no one can solve our personal problems for us. Each person, in this sense, must bear his own load or burden.

Jesus' message that the Kingdom of God is near implies that the potential for change is already given to the individual as God's gift. Jesus solved no problems for anyone. He was a catalyst, through which people became aware of their own indigenous resources that were often dormant, blocked, obscured, or repressed, in need of being coaxed out to the surface. God's liberator points to the Saving Possibility already present, waiting to be appropriated through repentance or similar decision. That's all anyone can do "for" us. Another human can bear our deepest personal burdens with us, but not for us, as far as personal change is concerned.

How did Jesus point to these already-present gifts in people? Sometimes by example. Through confrontation with his life, people transposed into the key of their own lives, saying, "Why, that's my possibility, too . . . to accept life as good in all of its yes and no . . . to be intensely involved in life, yet free for life . . . to care about other human beings, even when to do so clashes with my own vested interests." By sharing the sufferings and wrongs of others, Jesus held forth the possibility of personal change. In so doing, Jesus affirmed the worth of people when they had been wrong and when they had been wronged. By confronting people with a decision about their lives, Jesus brought to the surface a possibility of change. Sometimes this call to decision came as an abrupt awakening. This is at least part of the meaning of the story in John 5 which portrays the healing of a man who had been ill for thirty-eight years by the pool. Jesus confronts the man with the direct question, "Do you want to be healed?"

Just as no one can solve your problems for you, it is likewise true that you cannot solve anyone else's problems for him. You cannot live someone else's life for him. If we were mindful of this truth, we would be much less likely to resort to unnecessary advice-giving to others in times of their grief. One of life's most difficult demands is to accept the fact that some people will choose death over life, life negation over life affirmation. It is the false prophet who promises to solve other people's problems for them. This promise is the denial of the self-hood of others, and is, in fact, an attempt to take charge of other persons' lives. Bear one another's burdens, yes. But remember that each man must also bear his own burden and take responsibility for his life and his relationship to others.

The second basic assumption related to pastoral care implied from these Galatians passages is that no one can solve his own problems apart from community. If we believe this, we will be more likely to avoid "under-bearing." No one else can be you, but neither can you be yourself by yourself. The gospel steers us away from the "over-bearing" of "let us solve your problem for you," and away from the "under-bearing" of "every man for himself." We cannot bear other people's burdens for them, but it is equally true that none of us can bear our burdens without the care and interest of others. Tillich said that "care is universally human," that no one can take care of himself in every respect, that no one can even speak to himself without having been spoken to by others.[12]

True community reflected through pastoral care is neither a smothering dependence, nor a neglectful independence, but an interdependence through

[12] Paul Tillich, "The Theology of Pastoral Care," *Pastoral Psychology*, 1959, 10:21.

which we become ourselves in relationship to others. The community can affirm the worth and dignity of the individual, and hold up mirrors through which we can see ourselves more clearly. Particularly in times of loneliness, suffering, and sorrow, the Christian community can see to it that a person is neither neglected nor smothered, but extended the caring and sharing of the community of hope, through which that individual can experience the re-creation of his life. Every man must bear his own burden, but no man can bear it alone or unaided. The law of Christ is fulfilled through sharing the burdens of others and in allowing your own burdens to be shared.

As Bishop James Thomas once put it, we all live within our own "autobiographical shells." We cannot develop that shell apart from the strength, the insights, and the care which come to us from others as agents of the ultimate grace and love. One of the hidden problems of many persons is the narcissistic shell which makes it so difficult for us to *receive* help from others. To allow others to extend a ministry of pastoral care to us means we need to admit our interdependence, we need to trust others, and we need to risk ourselves in opening our wounds and perhaps laying bare our soul.

The alert and caring ministry of pastoral concern, whether through clergyman or layman, will neither smother nor neglect, but will offer support and assistance in order to free our neighbor for God, himself, and for others.

Sensitizing the Ministry of Lay Pastoral Care

As might be expected, educators in the field of pastoral care have had a variety of opinions concerning the respective roles of clergymen and laymen. Some writers have attempted to differentiate between pastoral care and helping acts, or between pastoral counseling and pastoral conversation. In each case, the implication has been to distinguish between clergy and lay roles, or at least between the trained and the relatively untrained, whether ordained or lay.

Along these lines I am confident of two matters relating to pastoral care. One is that laymen can do anything clergymen can do *if* they have equivalent training. Once the training is a reality, differences in pastoral care ability are a matter of the individual, not whether he is ordained or not. My second conviction is that, while only a few laymen will be involved in very intensive, long-range training, there are methods of sensitizing and developing the pastoral skills of many laymen. Generally speaking, these methods fall into two broad categories: a) those methods utilizing in a self-conscious way the insights, methods, and wisdom of Clinical Pastoral Education; b) more informal, less intensive means of training.

The use of Clinical Pastoral Education (CPE) in training laymen for their ministry of pastoral care is still a pioneer movement in local churches. Its proper functioning presupposes the presence of laymen who are willing to devote themselves to the training process, and the presence of a pastor or qualified leader who himself has experienced CPE as part of his own training. As I have suggested, I think it is accurate to say that CPE in local churches is a slowly emerging emphasis, concurrent with the lay renaissance and with the increased number of seminary students who are involved in CPE themselves.

In most cases, CPE in local churches is launched by the organization of a small group, carefully selected by the pastor. The CPE methods may include instruction, use of tapes followed by discussion, critical review of visits or interviews involving the trainees, oral or written reports, and case studies. Usually, CPE will involve small group interaction which fosters personal growth, and the focusing on one problem, such as visitation to hospital patients, elderly persons, or other people with special needs.

The necessary ingredients of quality CPE include the increase of theological understanding, an elementary grounding in personality dynamics, and a sharper awareness of the mission of the church. CPE is likely to be a process of several months, and will hopefully offer a learning opportunity through interpersonal relationships. Some laymen report that the most exciting aspect of CPE is their own increasing self-awareness as persons, accompanied by an awakening personal identity and sensitivity to others.

As a result of CPE, and sometimes of less intense or formal means of training, a great variety of lay pastoral ministries come into being. A United Methodist church in Houston, Texas, trained ten laymen in a four-month program centering around a ministry to eighteen families.[13] The ten met twice month-ly for instruction, visits with the families, and for evaluation of their ministry. In another urban area an ecumenical pastoral institute offered an eight-week course entitled "The Laymen as Counselor." Local clergymen and other professional persons from the community worked with several laymen to de-velop their "informal" counseling skills. Another seminar dealt with the basic elements of hospital visitation.

In *Basic Types of Pastoral Counseling*, Howard J. Clinebell, Jr. mentions a number of lay pastoral min-istries in process.[14] We note that these supportive and caring ministries are extended to both church members and those who otherwise have no relation-ship to the church. Pastoral care teams composed of laymen have offered a variety of ministries in dif-ferent locales. For example, these groups sponsor a ministry of acceptance, jobs, and housing for homeless alcoholics; visit the elderly, those in prison, juvenile courts, and children's homes; work in suicide-prevention centers as telephone counselors; and offer concern and support to the bereaved. This last function was developed through a downtown church in Minneapolis by training forty-two persons in the principles of helping the bereaved. Their min-istry includes a community of concern at the initial

[13] Robert C. Gentry, *Educating Laymen for a Ministry of Pastoral Care: An Application of Clinical Pastoral Education Methods in a Parish Setting*, Unpublished S. T. M. Dissertation, Perkins School of Theology, S. M. U., April, 1969.
[14] Pp. 284-87.

time of grief, as well as follow-up contacts for several months.

Where it does not seem feasible or possible to utilize CPE in the local church, other means can be set forth to sensitize the pastoral awareness and skills of the congregation.

Within the Northaven United Methodist congregation we have tried to open ourselves to deepening relationships and mutual care in a number of ways. These include sermons, encounter groups, retreats, and expressions of concern by the pastor and lay members for individuals in that part of the worship service known as the "Concerns of the Church." [15] A climate of concern can be slowly developed as the faith community remembers weddings, funerals, illnesses, and other personal celebrations or needs of its members.

For example, on one Sunday I offered a sermon in which I briefly spelled out the importance of lay pastoral care, and some destructive and constructive ways of trying to be helpful to people. In the introduction to the sermon I invited the congregation to be a part of the sermon by discussing it as soon as I had finished, and by sharing with one another the kinds of things they had experienced in one way or another as being constructive means of support and assistance.

The response was lively and exciting. One woman spoke of the grief she had experienced in her

[15] Our retreats, involving some thirty persons for either 24 or 48 hours, have been, for quite a few, the most rewarding form of experience in terms of personal relationships and deepening care and trust.

divorce, and told of how one or two persons had been able to share that grief, although many others did not seem able to understand. Another woman said that she had been helped the most on those occasions when she had been asked to help someone else, because out of this came a sense of worth and of being useful. A man told how a former minister had called him upon hearing of his father's death, saying only, "I wanted you to know that I cared." One person emphasized the need to be supportive from day to day, and not just when there is crisis or special need.

Out of this sermon came the decision to offer, through our Academy of Continuing Education, three evening sessions for developing lay pastoral skills. This series, entitled "Supportive Relationships Through Lay Pastoral Care," met for two-and-a-half hours each evening and was attended by fourteen persons.[16] The content for each evening was as follows: Session 1—Why do people hurt and how may we respond? Session 2—Shared experiences in giving and receiving support. Session 3—The ministry of pastoral care within Northaven.

Participants were persons with a particular interest in sensitizing their own ability to minister to other human beings. Some were persons who had experienced severe grief in past times, and who were willing to share their own reflections about these experiences in this small group of concerned persons. Dr. Elisabeth Kubler-Ross of the University

[16] Thirteen of the fourteen participants were women, possibly reflecting the prevailing cultural myth that nurture or care is primarily a female function.

of Chicago tells us in her book *On Death and Dying* that her team of doctors and clergymen have learned about death and dying from terminal patients in a way otherwise impossible.[17] Likewise, we learned that some persons who have experienced great sorrow can enrich our understanding of the dynamics of grief related to various human losses.

In our third session, as indicated above, we were involved in a depth discussion of pastoral care within Northaven. In dealing with questions like, "How has care not come within Northaven as you had hoped?" or, "Where has care and support come from within Northaven?" we discovered vastly different experiences and expectations. Some felt Northaven to be an incredibly open and receptive community, while others had experienced it as very cold and seemingly unsupportive. A number of concrete suggestions were offered for the mutual encouragement of supportive relationships.

Perhaps one of the more significant steps that emerged was the formation of a small group, including the pastor, which will be working together on an ongoing basis. This group will attempt to be a pastoral team involved in several kinds of ministries, including personal visits and telephone calls to persons in need of support and concern from the community of Christ. Some of the ministries, of course, have already been taking place. The existence of a group, however, will leave less to chance, will serve as an intentional communication resource, and will make possible a "seeking" ministry as well as a "waiting" ministry.

[17] (New York: The Macmillan Co., 1969).

In the mutual sharing of pastoral care by clergy and laity, the church more faithfully becomes the People of God, the Servant Community, the New Humanity it was called to be. And in the process, clergy and laity see one another not as professional-unprofessional, as ordained-unordained, but as human beings who are capable and in need of both giving and receiving a love which is grounded in the Saving Possibility of God's unconditional love exemplified in Jesus Christ.

The Gospel as Humanization Affirmed
the prophethood of all believers

4

The gospel of the Saving Possibility, rooted in God's love as gift and demand, calls the community of Christ to a dual role in today's society. One of these roles is the humanization of persons in their *possibilities*. The other task is the humanization of persons in their *polarization*. Together these two endeavors involve the church in a confluence of liberation and reconciliation. The humanization of persons in their societal possibilities and in their ideological polarization constitutes the ongoing Christian "revolution" in society, and points to a liberation and a reconciliation based on both action and attitude. Too often, reconciliation has been interpreted to mean an unjust peace, the reinforcement of racist structures, agreement on issues, or simply the mutual liking of one another.

The Humanization of Possibilities

The humanization of persons in their possibilities is well summed up in the following passage from Isaiah (58:6-12):

> Is not this the fast that I choose:
> to loose the bonds of wickedness,

to undo the thongs of the yoke,
to let the oppressed go free,
and to break every yoke?
Is it not to share your bread with
the hungry,
and bring the homeless
poor into your house;
when you see the naked, to cover him,
and not to hide yourself from your
own flesh?
Then shall your light break forth
like the dawn, and your healing
shall spring up speedily;
your righteousness shall go before you,
the glory of the Lord shall be your
rear guard.
Then you shall call, and the Lord will
answer;
you shall cry, and he will say,
Here I am.
If you take away from the midst of you
the yoke,
the pointing of the finger, and
speaking wickedness,
if you pour yourself out for the hungry
and satisfy the desire of the afflicted,
then shall your light rise in the darkness
and your gloom be as the noonday.
And the Lord will guide you continually,
and satisfy your desire with good things,
and make your bones strong;
and you shall be like a watered garden,
like a spring of water,
whose waters fail not.
And your ancient ruins shall be rebuilt;
you shall raise up the foundations of
many generations;

you shall be called the repairer of the breach,
the restorer of streets to dwell in.

Elsewhere, Isaiah refers to God's mission—as well
as that of his servant community—as good tidings
to the afflicted, the binding up of the brokenhearted, and the release of those who are oppressed.
(Isaiah 61) The New Testament repeats these passages from Isaiah in order to define the life and work
of Jesus, and thus of his body of followers, the community of Christ. (Luke 4:18-19) What does this
mean for you and me . . . and for the Christian
community today?

I have come to think that a sentence in a corporate prayer often used by our congregation sums it up
as well as anything I have heard. It goes like this:
*"We accept our common lot with all the hungry,
the frustrated, the wounded, the isolated, and the
insulted people of this world for the sake of our
common redemption."* I expect to agonize over
this "acceptance of our common lot" for the rest
of my life, because the key question for the church
in our generation is how and to what extent will
we accept our common lot with the outcasts and
the downtrodden in a mutual celebration of existence and a deepening of human relationships.

The acceptance of our common lot cannot legiti-
mately be a peripheral or optional matter for the
community of Christ. This claim is basic to the
very fabric of the gospel, as evidenced by the recurring New Testament emphasis on God's concern
for those of low degree, on Jesus' identification
with those who are oppressed and suppressed, and

on the early church's challenge of irresponsible use of power.[1]

No Christian celebration of the gospel has integrity unless it is celebration with cerebration, that is, an awareness, and even an agony, over the suffering of God's world. No Christian education is finally authentic until and unless somehow it leads to a deepening of concern for others. No Christian community is true, even to itself, unless its reason for being is to accept its common lot with the hungry, the naked, and the imprisoned. Is it not through these that Christ assured us we would find our common redemption? (Matthew 25:31-46)

The acceptance of our common lot is the quintessence of Christian vocation. Baptism, for most Christians today, is probably regarded as an innocuous ecclesiastical indoor sprinkling system. Baptism's real meaning includes initiation into our identification with all mankind. Confirmation is too often treated as joining a Christian club, whereas it should be clear that this is our acceptance of our common lot. With confirmants and with prospective adult members, we should make clear the implications of identification with the community of Christ. Do you see these people in our mental hospitals? Do you see the hungry, the ill-housed, the disadvantaged? See those in trouble and those who have no power of self-determination? Are you sure you want to accept your common lot with all of these? Because that is what you are signing up for! This is the life-style for which you are committing yourself.

[1] For some samples, see Luke 1:46-56; Matthew 25:31-46; I Corinthians 1:18-30.

And the world will be saying to you, "Don't get mixed up with caring about all those people out there. That won't get you anywhere in this world!"

The challenge for the church today, above all, is to give expression to this new life-style by which we accept our common lot with the downtrodden of the world, by which we give shape and concretion to the "underdog" theology of the New Testament. For the peculiar agony of the church today is that it has become all too clear that we are near novices as individuals, families, and congregations in our basic and fundamental vocation: to accept our common lot with the minorities, with those who hurt the most, with those we are consciously or unconsciously treating as "non"-persons by our very privileged and affluent positions in a world of starvation and dehumanization.

The anatomy of accepting our common lot is well spelled out, for the most part, in James Cone's *Black Theology and Black Power*. Because Black Power is an identification with the suffering poor, the reality of Black Power is indispensable to Christ's message to twentieth-century America, according to Cone. If the church denies this, it will become exactly what Christ is not. The real Church of Christ is that community which identifies with the suffering of the poor by becoming one with them. In this sense, the church must become black and brown and red and yellow in its direction and priority development.

"The church," says Cone, "must become prophetic, demanding a radical change in the interlocking structures of this society." [2] In other words, "men should be reminded of the awesome political responsibility which follows from justification by faith. To be made righteous through Christ places a man in the situation where he too, like Christ, must be for the poor." [3] Since the gospel is concerned for the liberation of man, so must be the community which bears that gospel. And it is liberation from injustice and oppression that characterizes Black Power.

All of this means that whites who would become black—which in this sense means those who are for the oppressed and poor of whatever color—need to look through the lens of so-called black theology to have an accurate understanding of today's situation between church and society. For example, integration can only mean that men of different races meet one another on equal footing, not on white terms. Reconciliation in a racist society "can be made a reality only when white people are prepared to address black men as *black* men and not as some grease-painted form of white humanity." [4] The lens of black theology forces us to see that white violence is and has been a systemic disorder in America for centuries, meaning that our insistence on "nonviolence" from minority people may be just another verbal alarm designed to protect white racism. For blacks, to love the white neighbor means "that the black man *confronts* him as a Thou without any intentions of giving ground by becoming an It. There-

[2] P. 2.
[3] *Ibid.*, p. 46.
[4] *Ibid.*, p. 147.

fore, the new black man refuses to speak of love without justice and power." [5] These are the kinds of signs and signals about which we must be clear if we are to truly accept our common lot with the world as it is.

Some tentative profiles of the "common lot" lifestyle would thrust in these directions:

1. Unless we are continually open to change in our own attitudes, we are deceiving ourselves in even talking about identifying with the poor and oppressed. The "Negro problem" is essentially in those of us who are white, not in black people. Failure to see this can result only in our continued dehumanization of ourselves and others.

2. In the complexity of today's changing world, knowledge is power. Again and again we find that even when we want to be the church in the world, we must have knowledge of complicated community issues and power structures. Even to support people creatively in their personal dilemmas presupposes some understanding of personality dynamics. Today, love without knowledge is more severely limited than ever before. Continuing education is a premium tool for us as individuals and as a Christian community concerned for the world.

If we are going to change the local prison or jail system, we must do our homework related to the political picture and the economic situation, and, most of all, deal with the attitudes in the community which have brought about our archaic systems. If we choose to become involved in help-

[5] *Ibid.,* p. 53

ing persons who are unjustly evicted by unreasonable landlords, we will have to do our homework. Knowledge is the beginning of power. And power rightly used is an instrument of love and justice.

3. For many persons, their "vocation within their vocation" (their employment as understood through a Christian life-style or calling) offers key opportunities for humane change. It has been among my deepest rewards as a clergyman to be associated with liberated business and professional men and women who view their work not only as a professional opportunity, but also as a means of a servanthood ministry to mankind. If the church is even going to begin to penetrate the urban developments in our nation which have so many built-in economic, social, and political injustices, a great deal of business and professional expertise will be needed.

4. For individuals to take seriously the acceptance of our common lot, it may mean the decision to become knowledgeable and responsible in a specific area of commitment, such as housing, preschool cooperatives with minority people, prison reform, or educational priorities. These choices are particularly imperative where people hold jobs that offer unusually limited opportunities related to the humanization of society. That is, if one's job provides an extremely limited base for a servant ministry, it becomes all the more important to find possibilities outside the job. The means of specialized commitment can be task groups organized through the church or by involvement in other existing community organizations. Many congregations today

serve as information and recruitment centers for specialized areas of commitments.

5. How many families imagine themselves as a missional community? Even many persons who have grown up in the church have seldom thought of their families in other than the cultural terms of "getting ahead, keeping up with the Joneses, and seeking their own advantage and comfort." Today's nuclear family tends to be isolated from the needs of the world, from a richness which comes from variety, and from its own true center of profound possibility. What does it mean for families to see their existence in terms of an extended family in the sense of extending themselves in behalf of mankind? What does it mean for families to realize how impoverished they are without contributions from other cultures, especially in family life-styles?

A missional profile for a family would proceed through this kind of mutual agonizing: What does it mean for husband and wife to enable each other to give to the world? What kind of sacrifices do they make so that both can "do their thing" for humanity? How do we intentionally utilize our financial resources for the deepest needs of the world? What kind of priorities do we set as goals for our family which make possible a redeeming, serving family community?

Some families deliberately choose to live in a biracial neighborhood for the sake of their children and of themselves. This is their witness for a new ethic of residence. Another family intentionally gave up extensive traveling and instead used the money for desperate community needs. A husband began to spend more hours with the children so his wife could make it through her program of graduate studies in social work. By mutual decision, a husband and wife declined a promotion and move offered to the husband because their responsibilities in their local fair-housing project were too significant.

These images are, of course, merely suggestive of the style of question-asking and decision-making for families who take seriously their "common lot" in the world. Perhaps happiness is a family dedicated to the life-style of serving the *human race,* rather than the *rat race* of putting as much distance between ourselves and "the unwelcome society" as we can. The former is true celebration of life. The latter is a sad impoverishment of human beings.

Increasing numbers of affluent whites (some old and quite a few young) are waking up to the fact that we have been playing the wrong game with our lives. We have been more concerned with getting ahead than with accepting our common lot. The drama of today's local congregation is being played out on this question: how will you accept your oneness with all of God's people? That's where the agony is for the church today. That's where the conflict is. And that's where the ecstasy is. For, after all, God chose what is foolish in the world to shame the wise. Do we live by that? God chose what is weak in the world to shame the strong. Is that our life-style? God chose what is low and despised—I repeat—low and despised in the world to bring to naught the things that are (I Corinthians 1:27-28). Can we forget that Christ was born in a crib . . . in a manger . . . and lived as a carpenter . . . whose triumphal entry was on a common donkey . . . and who was crucified between two thieves . . . and whose new body as the community of Christ was born in the grave?

Our role as the community of Christ, then, is the humanization of persons in their possibilities. We can only participate in God's liberating mission as we accept our common lot with the misery of the world. Can there be any doubt that this means risk, conflict, and even polarization in the name of the God who loves both justice and mercy? For the church to sound off about Saving Possibilities without seeking to be an instrument of these Saving Possibilities is the most diabolical apostasy conceivable.

The basic intent of humanizing persons in their possibilities by accepting our common lot is the decrease of exploitation and the increase of justice and freedom for all people. The accomplishment of this goal presupposes a political gospel which seeks the creation of new structures for human dignity and self-determination. As Frederick Herzog worded it, the political gospel "differs from the social gospel in that it does not try to cure all the ills of society . . . it focuses on the severest social strain, namely, on political oppression." [6]

Above all, we need to be clear that humanization is *not* simply modernized technology which manipulates both the environment and human beings in it. We may need less technology, and certainly we need more controlled technology, if we are to sur-

[6] "The Political Gospel," *The Christian Century,* November 18, 1970, p. 1382.

vive pollution. Nor is humanization a synonym for correcting underdevelopment, although it might include development of resources for the well-being of the oppressed. The so-called underdeveloped countries are less developed in uncontrolled technology, superficial ideas of success, use of violence, and many other characteristics of so-called developed countries.

By humanization we should mean the increase of self- determination, and the increase of the necessities and decencies of life for all people, and the increase of choices for life-styles and opportunities. In other words, the task of humanization is not to be construed as the desire to increase the American way of life or the Western way of life. Humanization is liberation from the social structures of poverty and powerlessness. But it is also emancipation from the mental structures which enslave men of all races in the chains of racism, misuse of power, and death through lovelessness.

The community of Christ must, of course, recognize that abundant life is possible, even amidst suffering and injustice. As William Stringfellow has said, there is more life and soul in some Harlem residents than in many affluent suburbanites. The affluent may be in greater need of liberation than the poor because the affluent are imprisoned by tyrannical assumptions. If we allow less than desirable circumstances to keep us from "living our lives" now, our lives always exist in some future possibility which may or may not come to pass. Yet we must equally realize the degrading efforts of hunger, lack of opportunity, and inhuman living

146

conditions. We cannot let the call to live fully in the now blind us to our responsibilities to be agents of a more just and humane future.

The Christian community must say, "Live now," and at the same time realize that oppressive social conditions have a way of taking their toll on the self-images and personal potential of children, youth, and adults. These social conditions are our imperatives to change the future, which is always becoming the present. Jesus proclaimed the breaking in of the Kingdom of God *now*. It is already in your midst. But this coming of God's Kingdom or rule brought with it the demand of a risk-filled mission to our neighbors for the sake of our common redemption.

The idea that "you can live your life now," combined with responsibility for shaping a new future, is a vital balance of the Christian gospel. Without the former, our false god becomes the best efforts of men to build a better world. And if our efforts to make the world "work" are miserable failures, what then? Yet without the demand to participate in the misery of the world, the insistence that you can live fully now is rightfully denounced as an irresponsible cop-out.

Speaking from the context of the freedom fighters in Zambia (Rhodesia), Colin Morris reflects on the condition of so many of the world's peoples in our day. "Those who preach Justification to them—that it is God's grace rather than their own efforts which saves them—have little idea of the spiritual demoralization and utter despair that numb the re-

sponses of those who hang on to life by a thread." [7]
Let all beware who preach grace as cheap grace—
as grace which does not have firmly implanted
within it a cruciform command to alleviate human
suffering. For God's Saving Possibility (Revelation)
always brings with it God's Revolution—the humanization of possibilities. We cannot give a deaf ear
to those who claim that reliance on the grace of
God has been an alternative to summoning men to
better the condition of their neighbors, that the
grace of God is a sleeping pill, that Christians are
guilty of quietism. There is too much evidence in
Christian history that these claims are legitimate
warnings.

The Humanization of Polarization

In the opening paragraph of this chapter, I suggested that the church has a dual role in today's
society. We have reflected on one of them: the
humanization of persons in their *possibilities*—attitudinal, imaginal, political, economic, social. Now
we turn to the second role, that of the humanization of persons in their *polarization*. Simply put,
our task as the church is not only to identify with
the oppressed and the downtrodden, but to do so
in a way which humanizes the polarization increasingly characteristic of our nation.

We are caught in the grip of a demonic process
which diminishes our capacity to see persons as
human beings. Especially is this true if their ideology

[7] *Unyoung, Uncolored, Unpoor,* p. 147.

of life disagrees with our own. Even though the term "polarization" implies separation and distance, it does not have to mean dehumanization of people. It is not, in fact, the polarization of ideas or ideology as such that constitutes sickness unto death or cultural cancer. Widely divergent ideas are characteristic and even necessary to the freedom and plurality which democracy presupposes.

It is the diminution of our capacity to see our ideological opponents as human beings that endangers democracy and degrades life, not polarization per se. Although polarization is defined by some as meaning inherent dehumanization, I do not think this definition goes to the root of our problem. Polarization means a sharp division or contrast, but does not necessarily mean relating to others as though they were less than human beings. *That* is the real problem in our midst.

I suppose there is really no new form of prejudice in the world, since all possible shapes and nuances have been practiced by the human race in the long development of our history. But there seems to be in American society an "in" prejudice which now accompanies the well-known fact of racial prejudice. I'm speaking of a prejudice which asserts itself because of the color of a man's ideas or the priorities of the group by which he is identified. Instead of seeing human beings, we see only an extension of those people through their ideas or their groups. This increasingly popular prejudice, with devotees on both the political right and left, is the creator of the New Nigger in American society. Of course, this is, in reality, an old-fashioned prejudice now applied to increasing numbers of people.

On the one hand (the right hand) those who have opposed our foreign policy and our Asian war have been frequently stereotyped with simplistic labels. From the highest ranking political offices in the nation to many newspaper editorials, this cheap and cavalier stereotyping has been escalated across the nation. Peace advocates are labeled intellectual snobs, lefty q. liberal, rotten apples, and other labels of a *personna non grata* nature. These labels in and of themselves are, of course, harmless, and are part and parcel of the traditional American political scene. Yet, the scorn and derision with which these labels are used are symptomatic of a dangerous dismissal of the humanity or personhood of those who are so simplistically labeled. This spiraling stereotyping adds nothing to intellectual understanding of the issues, and feeds the roots of suspicion, paranoia, and emotional bitterness which are abundantly present without being further inflamed by sloganmongers. When we begin to think of our political opposites as homogeneous blobs or nonpersons, we no longer have to take them seriously as human beings.

In *The Arrogance of Power,* Senator J. William Fulbright puzzles over the ability of so many people to think in terms of destroying huge numbers of other human beings, like "bombing Hanoi back to the Stone Age." [8] He comments that most of these persons would not think of refusing aid to a sick

---

[8] (New York: Vintage Books, 1966), p. 165.

child or a neighbor in need. They live their lives as decent people, not as barbaric warmongers. Yet as they begin to think of the enemy as a homogeneous, impersonal blob, they become victimized by the inhuman tendency of a willingness to destroy entire cities and nations.

Through a similar process of dehumanization, many Americans who have been deeply convinced of the wrongness and the immorality of our actions in Vietnam have become the New Nigger in the minds of their fellow citizens. Not because of the color of their skin or their race, but because of their ideas. This, of course, does not mean that the New Nigger experiences the across-the-board deprivation known for so long by so many minority persons. It simply means he is dismissed as a person, and to that limited extent is thereby dehumanized.

On the other hand (the left hand), there are those on the opposite end of the political spectrum who have been busy creating their own list of New Niggers. One does not have to have a "pro-police" attitude to raise the questions: "Is a man a pig because he wears a dark uniform, any more than a black man is a nigger because his skin is dark? Is a man to be judged guilty by association, or by the fact that he is in a certain occupation?" Those of us who are vigorously opposed to police brutality and increasingly questionable forms of repression should likewise oppose the dehumanizing, niggerizing, or homogenizing of policemen by hordes of chanting protestors who mesmerize the police with crescendos of insults, taunts, and obscenities.

Americans who take to the streets have every

right to protest, but when protesters deliberately harass public servants, no matter how irresponsibly some of these men in uniform may have performed in the past, then a prejudice is being ventilated which is just as misguided, and similarly dehumanizing, as prejudice forced on minority groups throughout American history.

When we deliberately dehumanize our fellow citizens, and purposely stereotype them, regardless of their individuality, we are working for strife, anarchy, and repression, not justice, peace, or human understanding. When one group hurls insults and obscenities like "pig," "gestapo," and "fascist" at another group, they are putting into motion a self-fulfilling prophecy which drives their opponents toward the very position of which they are being accused. Those who are maligned are more likely to act like pigs than human beings because they have been treated more like pigs than human beings. They are not thereby excused, but neither can their tormentors wash their hands of the responsibility.

Policemen are not the only New Niggers created by the political left. I think I can safely say that there are few citizens who have greater misgivings than I concerning the rise of militarism in the United States.[9] Nevertheless, it is crucial for us to distinguish between militarism and individuals who are participants in the military system. If we don't, we are creating another New Nigger in our society, and the disease of prejudice spreads further. We

[9] I have expressed these concerns in the appendix of *Christ's Suburban Body,* co-authored with Wilfred Bailey (Nashville: Abingdon Press, 1970).

cannot rightly prejudge individuals just because they are part of a system with which we are in either partial or radical disagreement.

The real question for us to be dealing with is: "Do you have to have a Nigger?" And who will your Nigger be? Men in black skin; men in dark uniforms; the over-thirty; the under-thirty; the bearded ones; the smooth ones; the dissenters; the supporters? We as a nation are rapidly escalating a dehumanization in which anyone who belongs to a certain group or who has certain ideas (namely, ones we don't like) has become our newest Nigger.

As I reflect on our societal situation in America today, I see four choices before us. One is violence. It must be perfectly clear that long before a few contemporary blacks in our nation began to favor violence, white power had come and seen and conquered by violence. As a *Christian Century* editorial put it so well,

The bloody violence began with efforts to dispossess and exterminate Indians, moved on to the enslavement of black Africans, to violent revolution, to a national anthem which glories in the glare of rockets and the burst of bombs in the night, and in a religion of conquest, to civil war, to frontier lawlessness, to vigilante executions, to industrial hostilities, to mob lynchings, to imperial adventures in Latin America and the Pacific, to world wars, to atomic bombs, to assassinations, to organized crime, to urban chaos, to police riots, to napalm and antipersonnel weapons. Which is why H. Rap Brown said that "violence is as American as cherry pie." [10]

[10] Copyright 1970 Christian Century Foundation. Reprinted by permission from the September 9, 1970 issue of *The Christian Century*.

Although Colin Morris documents a substantial case for the use of violence by Christians in some circumstances (mercy may require revolution), it seems clear that, in our nation, violence by minority groups will surely bring greater repression and futility. As Morris himself says, "Badly directed violence may, at great cost in human life, give Authority an excuse to rid itself once and for all of thorns in its flesh." [11] The more we claim that violence is not the answer, however, the more we must seek to accept our common lot with all . . . the more we must insist that the system work for *all* of our citizens. The truth is that our propensity for violence increases in ratio to how much we are suffering due to violence already existing in systemic form. I doubt if any white man has the right to lecture any black man today on the morality of nonviolence.

A second route for our nation is to unify and to depolarize. Unfortunately, this is like saying to people, "Give up your convictions and sacrifice your own conscience for the sake of unity." Or, "Surrender your blackness and be white like us." Unity is a great goal, but it cannot be achieved in a democracy at the price of surrendering individual conscience or a new image of self-consciousness. Is it not obvious that a plurality of diverse ideologies is destined to be characteristic of an epoch of great change such as we are now experiencing? In the way in which I am using the term polarization, depolarization is not a possibility, and maybe not even a desirability.

[11] *Unyoung, Uncolored, Unpoor*, p. 91.

Thirdly, there is the path of a dehumanizing polarization, with its creation of New Niggers in the body politic right and left. This is a one-way street which leads to disaster. If this dehumanizing polarization continues to spread, it may not make much difference in the long run what your position is on foreign policy, or law and order, or on fiscal priorities for the nation. Under an unrelenting assault of niggerizing one another, the genius of the democratic idea—respect for the individual, or at least for his rights, if not for his opinions—will erode away until the land is possessed by demons of fear, repression, and revenge.

Our fourth possibility is to humanize—not remove —but humanize the polarization. By treating our ideological opponents as persons rather than things, persons with hopes and hurts, agonies and anxieties, potential and promise. By communicating humanness in the midst of conflict. By seeing a human being behind the ideas which we believe to be mistaken. By avoiding the stereotyping of those with whom we are in radical disagreement. By not falling into the trap of creating New Niggers. By not claiming more for our position than we can truly claim.

It is this fourth choice—the humanization of polarization—to which the gospel calls us. Along with the humanization of possibilities, this humanization of polarization constitutes the shape of the Christian revolution. This ongoing and permanent revolution in every age is one by which men are called to respond and relate to one another as human beings, not as "non"-persons. The task of the Christian revolution, then, is to identify with

155

the oppressed and the downtrodden, but to do so in a way which points through the event of Jesus as the New Being to that humanness common to all people.

Whenever, in the name of supposedly humanitarian revolution, we begin to make the revolution more important than human beings, then we have forsaken the Christian revolution and revelation for a counterfeit movement. Jürgen Moltmann makes this point well in *Religion, Revolution, and the Future* when he outlines Camus' description of the humane principle of revolution:

The slave revolts against his master. He denies him as a master, but not as a man. For his protest is directed against the master's refusal to treat him as a man. As master and slave, neither is a true man and neither can relate to the other in a humane way. If the denial of the master were total, the slave's revolt would bring nothing new into the world but would only exchange the roles of inhumanity. The humane revolution, however, is not out to turn the slaves into masters, but to subvert and abolish the whole master-slave relationship so that in the future men will be able to treat one another as men. If the revolution loses sight of this goal, it becomes nihilistic and forfeits its fascination.[12]

Humanizing the polarization requires more of us than any of the other alternatives—violence, false unity, or dehumanizing polarization. Where there cannot be reconciliation of ideological differences, the reconciliation for which we work is that of seeing

[12] (New York: Charles Scribner's Sons, 1969), pp. 142-43.

and relating to others as persons rather than things. This is what James Cone is pointing to when he speaks of blacks relating to whites in a Thou-to-Thou manner instead of a Thou-It way. The gospel calls us to be the harbingers of humanization in today's polarization.

Finally, we must recognize that these dual roles of the church in society will result in a creative tension in behalf of a better world. Role one—the humanization of attitudinal, social, educational, and especially political possibilities will bring about conflict and an inevitable deepening of polarization in the name of justice and self-determination. As a matter of fact, we see this polarization throughout the New Testament narrative. Wherever Jesus went, there was sharp division of opinion. Some said he was an enemy of the people. Others said he was the Messiah, the ultimate truth.

Jesus proclaimed the love of God as a gift to all who would receive it. In other words, even those who opposed him were regarded as human beings, not as objects. This is the basis for the second role of the Community of Christ—the humanization of polarization. The Christian revolution, then, is concerned not only with the rights of the oppressed, but also for both oppressed and oppressor as persons. The humanization of persons in both their possibilities and in their polarization is called forth by the love of God revealed in Jesus Christ, and at the same time points to the love in which all human endeavor is grounded and sustained.

The Gospel as Death Affirmed
the ultimate resurrection

5

Charlie Brown spoke for all of us when he said, "I'm too me to die." Fear of death is indeed, to one degree or another, a universal fear. In fact, in our own unconscious we cannot conceive our own death, but only the death of others.[1] Death represents uncertainty about the future, loss of all relationships, and the threat of nonbeing. Our fear of death in American society has been well documented again and again by highly descriptive accounts of our evasions and euphemisms in the face of death.[2] These attempts to avoid and ignore the reality of death are so recognizable to those who wish to see them that they need no elaboration here.

Not only is fear of death a virtually universal phenomenon, but there is also what Paul Tillich called anxiety of fate and death, that is, the state in which a being is aware of its possible nonbeing. "It is not the realization of universal transitoriness, not even the experience of the death of others, but the impression of these events on the always latent awareness of our own having to die that pro-

---

[1] Kubler-Ross, *On Death and Dying*, p. 2.
[2] Two well-known examples are Evelyn Waugh's *The Loved One* and Jessica Mitford's *The American Way of Death*.

duces anxiety. Anxiety is finitude, experienced as one's own finitude." [3] For Tillich it was the anxiety of not being able to preserve one's own being which underlies every fear and is the frightening element in it. He saw the anxiety of death as one of the three kinds of anxiety which belongs to existence itself.

The Inadequacy of Secular and Religious "Answers" to Death

I believe that Christian faith has profound resources for facing the reality of death, whether we speak of the specific fear of death or in broader terms of the anxiety of non-being. However, these implications are not necessarily the usual ones espoused by secular or by religious interpretations. Neither the traditional Christian assurances of personal post-death survival nor the present fascination with various dimensions of psychic research into "life beyond" do justice to the deepest questions related to man's life, death, and destiny. The same can be said in reference to the practice of cryogenics by which bodies are put in deep freeze awaiting later scientific resuscitation.

These usual "answers" from both religious and secular sources are concerned only with a quantitative interpretation of man's being, with assurance of an endless span of life. They provide no help whatsoever nor shed any illumination on the problem of the quality or purpose of man's life and death. Indeed, if anything, they obscure the real essence

[3] *The Courage to Be* (New Haven: Yale University Press, 1952), p. 35.

of man's reason for being. They evidence no interest in coming to grips with *the* problem of life which is the problem of love.

To be sure, I am very convinced that "whether we live or whether we die, we are the Lord's." (Romans 14:8) This is to say that God's love embraces our life and our death and that we forever belong in his life. I am content to leave open exactly what this means, whether some kind of subjective or else an objective kind of immortality. I'll say more on this later. The point I wish to make here is that the popular "answers" to death provided by both secular and religious groups do not fundamentally deal with the basic issue of how man shall live his life and die his death and for what purpose.

There is yet another sense in which the common preoccupation with post-mortem subjective existence fails to deal with the problem posed by death. As pointed out by Schubert M. Ogden, death is not merely a future reality yet to come, but is taking place now in the passing away of all our moments of experience.[4] The immediate and irreversible transience of all our experiences, which Alfred North Whitehead called "perpetual perishing," carries into a more and more remote past all our thoughts and feelings and actions. Thus, all our experiences continually recede into the void of the past almost as though they had never been at all.

What profit would it be for us to go on living— even to eternity—if the net result of all our having

---

[4] *The Reality of God;* see chapter 8, "The Promise of Faith."

lived were simply nothing; if our successive presence in no way added up to a cumulative accomplishment such as no creature is able to provide either for himself or for his fellows? This is the question that seems to me to expose the profound inadequacy of all the philosophical and theological theories of "subjective immortality" . . . the deeper problem of mortality, of the incessant passing away of whatever comes to be, is left completely unsolved and, indeed, is even intensified by all such theories.[5]

A Persuasive and Potent "Answer" to Death: The Reality of Love

Love is virtually always described in Christian thought as the very meaning and purpose of life. There are, of course, nuances of interpretation, but love in the Christian sense of agape will have a profile something like this: rooted in God's love or agape . . . affirmation of the created order and life as good gifts . . . active good will, undeserved and freely given . . . characterized by forgiveness, generosity, and concern for the well-being of others. The New Testament tells us that God is love and that we are to love others as he loves them and as he also loves us.

Now in the light of the primacy of love as the essence of true and abundant life, it is odd how seldom love is likewise mentioned as the surest antidote for our anxiety toward nonbeing or our fear of death. Why is love not also seen as the deepest and most potent way of relating to death,

[5] *Ibid.*, p. 225.

since death is an experience within life without which life is incomplete?

I believe that our most challenging and rewarding hope toward death is reflected in I John's belief—"We know that we have passed out of death into life because we love the brethren. He who does not love remains in death." (3:14) This approach to death has greater integrity and challenge than the fascination—one might almost say insistence!—with our subjective post-mortem life. All other theories or approaches to death are motivated by a quantitative search rather than a search for the qualitative possibilities presupposed in a deepening and maturing of love. Only the latter can equip man to accept his creatureliness as a good gift.

Love fulfills and frees the self by pointing beyond the self. Love affirms the deepest needs of the self, yet makes the center of the self more than the self. The Christian love ethic points beyond the self, beyond one's own family, class, race, state, nation, or any other limited circle. In terms of Charlie Brown's "too me to die," love does not negate one's me-ness, but rather fulfills one's me-ness by linking it to the life-giving source and all-embracing Whole of life.

Our relatedness to the Whole (God) through love expands our vision and our sense of being a meaningful part of the life process in several ways. For example, we can speak of life's ecology of death by which the continuation of the human race and the right to life of unborn generations depend on our death. In the actual facing of our own impending death, I fully realize that this future possibility of mankind is not likely to be a substitute for the various feelings of anger, hostility, and depression which so often belong to the dying person.

Yet, without minimizing the inevitable feelings bound up with our own dying, why should we not care deeply about the rights of others—for example, our children's children—to have life on this already overcrowded planet? And there can be little doubt that the life of future generations is not possible apart from the death of the preceding generation. Insofar as we do love God's world and affirm his gift of life, can we be completely oblivious to the right of others to have life, too?

To take a slightly different example of the possible power of love in relation to death, love makes the center of value God, or the Whole, instead of ourselves. Love challenges our tendency to make the self into the center of all that is, so that our contribution to the Whole becomes increasingly significant and the question of personal survival less important. As Erich Fromm has made clear in his writings, the hoarding mannerisms that come from selfishness are derived not from too much self-love, but from a dearth of authentic self-affirmation. Love liberates our me-ness *from* its self-imposed prison of fear and *for* a style of giving, generosity, and acceptance of value beyond the self.

Many Christians would do well to learn from our brothers in Reform Judaism. For them God or the Whole is loved not because he is the guarantor of subjective immortality, but because God is both the beginning or source of life and the end of life. In Christian thought, this foundation of a saving faith is reflected in the belief that we live and move and have our being, not finally in ourselves, but in God's everlasting love. Our life is from God, to God, in God, and for God. "There is one God, the Father, from whom are all things and for whom we exist." (I Corinthians 8:6)

Love, then, points beyond the self, embracing the Whole because the self is already embraced by the Whole. Whether I continue or not in a subjective or conscious sense, the reality in whom all life is sustained and nourished does continue—as it was in the beginning, is now, and ever shall be. The deeper question is, not how can I somehow manage to subjectively survive death (as much as I may desire that possibility), but how can I love God and the world of others who are also loved by God? Apart from love, do we not indeed remain in death, as I John claims? Is not our deepest liberation for life—and for death—the growth of love in our relationships? Is not our greatest journey that of learning to reach beyond ourselves and those who are like us to all those others?

In his book *The Greening of America*, Charles Reich of Yale unravels three levels of consciousness related to America's past, present, and future.[6] On a broader and different scale, it would seem that human beings have the possibility of experiencing three levels of consciousness. Consciousness I revolves around what seems best for me, around my needs for gratification. This is an infantile stage of development. All that matters is the meeting of my

[6] (New York: Random House, 1970).

needs. My needs *are* the world, so to speak. Everything is evaluated by how it affects me.

Consciousness II is an expansion of Consciousness I. Everything is now evaluated by how it affects my group—class, race, school, club, church, state, profession, nation. This level of being is the socialization of level I, and might loosely be thought of as an adolescent level of consciousness. All that counts is what affects me and my group.

In Consciousness III, the previous two are in a continual process of being replaced by a universal or cosmic consciousness. Its circle of reference is not merely the self, or the self and its similar peers. The framework has now become all men, the whole creation, all that is. De Chardin spoke of the "planetization" of the human spirit. Through the third level of consciousness, we experience the greening or maturing of life. This is what happens when God happens in our lives, when the love of Christ is epiphanied as event.

In this third or cosmic consciousness, there is a death and a birth. For it is indeed a death when the welfare of the human race becomes more important to us than our own standing in the so-called "rat race" of society against itself. But this death is likewise a birth. And what a birth! There is no other birth quite like it. For this universal or cosmic consciousness is a profound release, an at-one-ment with the world, a reconciliation with life. The center of Consciousness III is a love which frees the self for the self, yet for all others as well . . . and for the Whole in whom both self and other selves are embraced.

I'm convinced that for many Christians—as well as many who do not understand themselves through that label—the primary question is *how* can we learn to love? These persons have already accepted the primacy of universal love as an ideal. They have already accepted the idea that the real question for them is not how or whether they go on living endlessly as experiencing, subjective selves. Their real question is how can they love in spite of all their hang-ups and personal weaknesses . . . in spite of the competitive and impersonal society in which they live . . . in spite of the seemingly insurmountable indifference of the world in which they live.

It is not my purpose herein to dwell on factors that increase our capacities to grow in love of God, self, and neighbor. However, I will indicate briefly two matters which are central, convictions which are at least indicated in chapter 2. First, we can hardly expect to be able to be open and loving toward others unless and until we are open to God's love for us. God's love means that we are not on trial as human beings, that we do not have to prove ourselves as human beings in the eyes of others. We are already "okayed" by God's love. In traditional theological terms, I am speaking, of course, about justification by grace through faith.

If anything else other than the love of God is allowed to become the total source of our meaning and reason for being, we can be sure that a joyous affirmation of life will become all but impossible. Any other source of bread will prove itself to be inadequate, and we will find ourselves entangled in a web of self-defeating schemes and the disillusionments which inevitably accompany them. In a sense, it is God's love "against the field," that is, against all other possibilities and combinations thereof which offer themselves as a foundation for our self-understanding and our corresponding actions.

Second, the acceptance of God's love for ourselves cannot be set apart from our acceptance of God's love for our fellow human beings. The two are inseparable. Before we can truly affirm other human beings, we have to know that we are affirmed, and that likewise other persons are *worth* affirming and loving. In other words, we need to see others through God's love for them. To say this in a slightly different way, we need to judge others by God's grace toward them or love for them rather than by the human standard of how they affect us! Otherwise we slip into the narcissistic practice of placing ourselves in the middle of the universe and evaluating all others on the frightfully limited basis of how we are affected.

If we learned to relate to others through God's love, we would not be so blinded by whether or not other persons look like we think they ought to look, or act like we act. At least we might see them as human beings instead of dismissing them as hippies, Birchers, revolutionary leftists, Agnew lovers, or whatever. As Ramsey Clark has so clearly pointed out, people lose their compassion and even their reason when they become obsessed with fear. Perhaps if we allowed a bit more of God's love to permeate our lives, we would experience less fear and more concern and compassion.

I would be quick to admit—in fact, even to insist—that our capacity to recognize the love of God is influenced by a multitude of factors, including all of our experiences with our parents, our relationship to our peer group and the socialization process, and the cultural environment in which our formative years take place. These factors often seriously hamper the likelihood by which God's love becomes the redeeming reality in our lives. It is the task of the humanization process, sketched out in chapter 4, to increase the possibilities which shape our lives from the very beginning.

A child growing up in the slums in the absence of decent living conditions may seem to have little reference in his experience for either the term "love" or "God." But that can be equally true of the neglected offspring of $60,000-a-year suburban parents. There is no substitute for the presence of human love and care, yet these very forms of care can only point beyond themselves to the all-embracing love in which we live and move and have our being. It is God's love which constitutes the ongoing, unfolding epiphany of life in its totality. It is God's love which offers us a new beginning in spite of all our past mistakes. It is God's love which is the possibility-giver of all human love, and which is saying to us, "LIVE!"

As we consider how love is a persuasive and potent "answer" to death, I seek to clarify an important possible misunderstanding. Readings in the field of psychology suggest that what enables a person to grapple with death, especially when death becomes an immediate prospect rather than an intellectual concept, is how one feels about oneself. If a person feels a sense of accomplishment, a sense of ego-integrity, a sense of creative fulfillment in some essential way, then death can be struggled with more openly and affirmatively. I think there is probably a great deal of truth in these assertions. Although persons oriented toward behavioral psychology might not be comfortable with Christian categories, I do not think there has to be a conflict between feeling good about yourself and what I have been calling the reality of love.

In a reasonably "healthy" person, I suspect that good feelings about oneself come precisely out of having made some contribution to the health or happiness of others. Any such contribution may be "a personal achievement," but that does not, of course, necessarily make it a self-centered matter. Why shouldn't we receive pleasure and satisfaction from pursuits which enrich the lives of other human beings? Is this not precisely the mark of a mature person—that he receives pleasure from enterprises that enhance the lives of others rather than from so-called accomplishments that harm others? Or that more pleasure is received from activities that benefit others as well as oneself than activities that in some way benefit only oneself?

An illustration of these thoughts was afforded in an issue of *Psychology Today* which featured articles concerned with death. The editorial was a tribute to Abraham Maslow, a frequent contributor to the magazine who, just prior to his death, had sent the editors a tape about his personal thoughts on death.

Maslow talked with intense introspection about

an earlier heart attack that had come right after he completed an important piece of work. "I had really spent myself. This was the best I could do, and here was not only a good time to die but I was even willing to die. . . . It was like a good ending, a good close. I think actors and dramatists have that sense of the right moment for a good ending, with a phenomenological sense of good completion—that there was nothing more you could add. . . . Partly this was entirely personal and internal and just a matter of feeling good about myself, feeling proud of myself, feeling pleased with myself, self-respecting, self-loving, self-admiring. . . .

"My attitude toward life changed. The word I used for it now is the post-mortem life. I could just as easily have died so that my living constitutes a kind of an extra, a bonus. It's all gravy. Therefore I might just as well live as if I had already died.

"One very important aspect of the post-mortem life is that everything gets doubly precious, gets piercingly important. You get stabbed by things, by flowers and by babies and by beautiful things— just the very act of living, of walking and breathing and eating and having friends and chatting. Everything seems to look more beautiful rather than less, and one gets the much-intensified sense of miracles.

"I guess you could say that post-mortem life permits a kind of spontaneity that's greater than anything else could make possible.

"If you're reconciled with death or even if you are pretty well assured that you will have a good death, a dignified one, then every single moment of every single day is transformed because the pervasive undercurrent—the fear of death—is removed. . . . I am living an end-life where everything ought to be an end in itself, where I shouldn't waste any time preparing for the future, or occupying myself with means to later ends. . . .

"Sometimes I get the feeling of my writing being

a communication to my great-great-grandchildren who, of course, are not yet born. It's a kind of an expression of love for them, leaving them not money but in effect affectionate notes, bits of counsel, lessons I have learned that might help them. . . ." [7]

In my own judgment, too many Christians have been too quick to condemn good feelings about oneself. By the same token, behaviorists are frequently too quick to foreclose on the ground of grace which breathes through authentic human love and by which human love is sustained and enabled. Although Maslow's frame of reference was perhaps different from my own, his statement combines authentic feelings of self-love with an expression of love for others. Any Christian theology which cannot embrace that combination is a sick theology.

This part of the chapter has claimed that love fulfills and frees the self by relating the self beyond itself to a greater center of value (God) of which the self is a part. Now comes another assertion. *Love can make us aware that death is not the greatest threat to life.* If by life we mean only the *length* of life, then death would truly be life's greatest threat. But if by life we mean essentially the significance or quality of life, then it is unlived or loveless life that constitutes the greatest threat. Our lovelessness means, according to I John's viewpoint, that we are already "in death." As our life is from God and for God, the above assertion is all the more true.

We must choose which of these concepts of life is the most real to us. Martin Luther King, Jr. was

[7] From *Psychology Today* Magazine, August, 1970. Copyright © Communications/Research/Machines, Inc.

fond of saying that if there is nothing for which a man will put his life on the line, then the physical cessation of his heart is merely the belated announcement of a death which had already taken place. We live in a society which is much more concerned with quantity than with quality, with growth in terms of size and numbers than in terms of humanness and personal or societal maturation.

The same problem reveals itself in our attitude toward life and death. Once it becomes clear that lovelessness is the threat with which we must come to grips rather than the length of life, we can concentrate on affirmative living—now and in this world and in whatever circumstances are at hand. Dr. Elisabeth Kubler-Ross of Chicago has described her task as being "to help people live while they are dying." She was referring to patients experiencing terminal illnesses. But perhaps her statement applies to all of us. Our task is to enable ourselves and each other to live while we are dying, because living is also the process of dying.

Love's Struggle: Coming to Grips with Many Deaths

Life is a continuum between the no longer and the not yet, full of deaths, losses, separations. From the moment we are born, we proceed from one death or loss to another until the concluding reality of physical death. Thus, death is always in the midst of life, so that the life process is also the death process. The two are part of each other. Just as each moment is a moment of life, it is also a moment of death. The whole of life, as the philosopher Martin

Heidegger put it, is "being toward death." Life belongs to death and death belongs to life.

Therefore, when we speak of love as the most profound way of relating to life, we are at the same time speaking of relating to death. So the way we anticipate death will likely be similar to the way in which we have dealt with other inevitable losses . . . separation from loved ones, loss of job or status, physical impairment, divorce.

We have found that different patients react differently to such news (terminal prospects) depending on their personality makeup and the style and manner they used in their past life. People who use denial as a main defense will use denial much more extensively than others. Patients who faced past stressful situations with open confrontation will do similarly in the present situation.[8]

If we were fortunate enough to have been sustained in loving relationships as children, we learned to come to grips with various kinds of inevitable losses which come to all of us. The function of love, at least in part, is to provide the internal security "to let go." Love increases our instinct toward qualitative importance and increases security and fulfillment by which we can "let go." For life is a process of "letting go," and it is this struggle with a series of losses or deaths with which love must continually contend.

Perhaps there is blessedness in sorrow and grief (blessed are those who mourn) because these experiences can teach us that nothing is really ours and

[8] Kubler-Ross, *On Death and Dying*, p. 29.

that everything is God's. All of our personal pronouns are merely figures of speech. He who can accept the passing awayness of all things into God will experience the peace of God which passes all human understanding.

It is interesting to note that while love makes the facing of death more acceptable, the ever-present possibility of death also makes love more possible. Awareness of death provides an intense experience of love, as Rollo May notes:

> Some—perhaps most—human beings never know deep love until they experience, at someone's death, the preciousness of friendship, devotion, loyalty. Abraham Maslow is profoundly right when he wonders whether we could love passionately if we knew we'd never die.[9]

Love does not remove anxiety, but it is the source of the "courage to be" by which our anxiety can be affirmed and dealt with. Some of us have seen the celebrative banners with the saying of Thomas Merton which speaks to this point: "Anxiety is inevitable in an age of crisis like ours. Don't make it worse by deceiving yourself and acting as if you were immune to all inner trepidation. God does not ask you not to feel anxious, but to trust in him no matter how you feel."

The Affirmation of Death

The most profound affirmation of death is not through our overcoming it by a quantitative addition

---

[9] *Love and Will* (New York: W. W. Norton & Co., 1969), p. 102. See chapter 4, "Love and Death."

of more consciousness, whether through religious or secular devices. Our deepest reward and challenge is the ecstasy of a growing love for God, for the gift of being, and for our fellowman. This love is not necessarily a substitute for feelings of rejection, anger, and depression, nor for the various stages through which we are likely to pass in a terminal process of dying.[10] Nor, as I have indicated, is love some kind of abstract substitute for the joy and satisfaction of personal achievements and self-affirmation. Love embraces these feelings and attitudes, but is finally rooted in the One in whose love our final meaning and destiny are secure.

It is the "promise of faith"—that we are all embraced everlastingly by the boundless love of God—that constitutes the Saving Possibility in relation to death. Our participation in life and death through the reality of love—itself a possibility given by God—makes clear the *very reason* for our life and death—to celebrate the worth of the All-Inclusive Reality from whom and for whom we live and die and have our being. Our true life is only in relation to the Whole, in whose unending love our lives forever belong. This is the gospel's affirmation of death.

*

[10] See Elisabeth Kubler-Ross's *On Death and Dying,* in which Dr. Ross describes the stages which the dying patient usually experiences: denial and isolation; anger; bargaining; depression; and acceptance.